PET VET FIRST AID GUIDE

Leah Hill, DVM
Copyright © 2024 Pet Vet Products, LLC

About the Author

Originally from Melbourne, Australia, Dr. Leah Hill moved to the United States in 1990 and earned her veterinary degree from Iowa State School of Veterinary Medicine in 1999. In 2004, she purchased a veterinary clinic in Merced, California, where she quickly noticed a lack of local emergency services for pets. Understanding the stress pet owners faced when forced to drive over an hour during critical situations, Dr. Hill established a 24/7 emergency clinic to provide accessible care to her community.

She owned and operated the clinic until 2016, when she sold the practice, but continues to practice small animal medicine, regularly handling emergencies with the same dedication she's shown throughout her career.

Driven by her commitment to helping pet owners, she authored the Pet Vet First Aid Guide and created a specialized PetVet Medic First Aid Kit to equip people with the tools they need during emergencies when veterinary care may not be immediately available. Dr. Hill currently resides in Orange County with her husband, daughter, two yellow labs, and two cats.

Disclaimer

This book is not a substitute for professional veterinary care. You must consult with your veterinarian whenever your pet is unwell or injured. This book aims to assist in emergencies when you cannot reach a veterinarian promptly. We assume no responsibility for any outcomes that may result from the use of this book.

To save money on all your pet needs, see Dr. Hill's online store: www.petvetproduct.com.

 Pet Poison Helpline®: (855) 764-7661

 Your local veterinarian:

 Local emergency veterinarian:

Knowing how to provide first aid to your furry friend in an emergency is essential. This guide aims to provide you with the basic knowledge and skills needed to help your pet in an emergency until you can get them to a veterinarian.

A first aid kit is essential to ensure you are ready for a pet emergency. You can assemble your kit or buy a premade PetVet Medic First Aid Kit containing all the necessary items. For more information about the premade kit, designed and approved by Dr. Hill, visit www.petvetproduct.com.

Table of Contents

Chapter 1: Preparing for Emergencies

A first aid kit is essential to ensure you are ready for a pet emergency. You can either assemble your own or buy the premade PetVet Medic First Aid Kit containing all the necessary items for most emergencies. For more information about the premade kit, visit www.petvetproduct.com.

Keeping your pet calm during an emergency can be challenging, but minimizing the risk of further injury can ensure their safety. Here are some tips that may help:

1. Stay calm yourself: Your pet can sense your emotions, so it's essential to remain calm and composed.

2. Use a soothing voice: Speak to your pet softly to help keep them calm.

3. Use a carrier or leash: If your pet is anxious or agitated, keep them secure and prevent them from running away.

4. Provide distractions: Offer your pet toys or treats to help distract and calm them.

5. Avoid making sudden movements: Try to move slowly and avoid any action that could startle your pet.

6. Cover their eyes: Covering your pet's eyes with a towel or blanket can help them relax.

7. Use a muzzle to prevent being bitten.

   - Place a regular muzzle, if available, around the pet's nose and secure behind their head.

   - A dog leash can act as a muzzle.

How to Muzzle Your Dog

Diagram 1.1

1. Approach your dog calmly and gently.

2. Make a large loop with a leash, and then slip the loop over the dog's snout. Then tighten gently. Ensure the loop fits comfortably around the snout without causing discomfort or restricting the dog's breathing.

3. Cross the two ends of the leash under the dog's chin.

4. Take the loose ends under the dog's jaw and bring them up behind the ears. (Be gentle and avoid pulling too tightly.)

5. Securely tie or fasten the loose ends of the leash behind the ears, creating a snug fit that prevents the dog from removing the makeshift muzzle.

6. Double-check the tightness to ensure it is secure enough to prevent the dog from opening their mouth wide or biting, but not so tight that it causes discomfort or restricts breathing.

Restraint Techniques

Cats

Kitty Burrito

You can wrap a cat securely in a blanket or towel to provide comfort and make it easier to give medications or help prevent them from scratching and thrashing around if they are in distress.

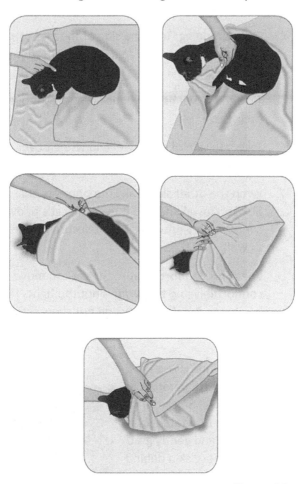

Diagram 1.2

1. Prepare a soft blanket or towel: Choose something that is large enough to wrap around the cat comfortably. Lay the blanket or towel on a flat surface.

2. Approach the cat calmly: To avoid startling them, speak softly and use soothing tones to keep the cat relaxed.

3. Gently pick up the cat and place them in the center of the blanket/towel, positioning them so that their body is parallel with the longer side of the fabric.

4. Start wrapping: Take the side of the blanket/towel closest to your cat's head and fold it under the chin to cover both front feet.

5. Take the towel behind your cat and lay it over the top of their back.

6. Take one side of the towel and wrap it over the cat's body, tucking it securely underneath the other layer.

7. Wrap the other side: Take the opposite side of the blanket/towel and fold it over the cat's body, crossing it over the previous fold. Tuck it securely underneath the cat as well.

8. Check for comfort: Ensure the cat can move their limbs comfortably and the wrap is not too tight. The cat should be able to breathe easily and not show signs of distress.

Scruff Restraint

The scruff technique is used when a cat is not cooperating or is being aggressive. Be careful not to get bitten or scratched. Go from behind and gently grab the scruff (the loose skin behind the head). Once you have the scruff, most cats will be calm.

Diagram 1.3

Stretch Restraint

This technique involves grabbing the scruff of your cat and laying them on their side. Then, with the other hand, extend their legs out.

 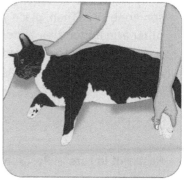

Diagram 1.4

Dogs

Restraint in Sitting Position

Place one arm under the dog's neck, and using the arm, hold the dog's head securely against your body. Place the other hand along their hind end to prevent them from standing up.

Diagram 1.5

Restraint in Standing Position

Place one arm under the dog's neck and use the arm to hold the dog's head securely against your body so they cannot bite you or someone else. Then, place your other arm under their abdomen up over the side to prevent them from sitting down or moving.

Diagram 1.6

Restraint in Lateral Position

While your dog is standing, reach over them and wrap your arms around them so that you can grasp the front leg and back leg closest to you. Keeping them tight against your body, lift their legs off the ground slowly, and use your body to guide them down gently. By holding onto the front and back leg closest to the ground, it prevents them from getting up. Your arm holding their front leg should be over their neck to prevent them from biting.

Diagram 1.7

Recommended Emergency Kit Items

- Flashlight
- Magnifying glass
- Porous tape (sports tape)
- 2" and 4" self-adhering bandaging material (vet wrap)
- Non-adherent sterile pads (2" x 3")
- Gauze pads (3" x 3")
- Combine ABD pads (5" x 9")
- 2" and 4" gauze roll bandage
- Cotton-tip applicators (10-pack)
- Silver rescue blanket
- Ice pack
- Heat pack
- Tweezers
- Collapsible water bowl
- Bandage scissors
- Nail clippers for dog
- Hemostats
- Tick remover
- Flea comb
- Thermometer
- Gloves
- 10 cc syringe
- Aluminum splint
- Glucose gel
- Liquid skin glue
- Saline flush
- Hydrogen peroxide
- Alcohol prep pads
- Triple antibiotic ointment
- Sterile eye lubricant
- Activated charcoal
- Hydrocortisone cream (1%)
- Burn cream or spray
- Electrolyte powder
- Dramamine (50 mg) or meclizine (25 mg)
- Benadryl* (25 mg)
- Wound clotting material

Visit www.petvetproduct.com to purchase the premade PetVet Medic First Aid Kit.

Make sure that the Benadryl you use does not contain xylitol.

Chapter 2: Choking and CPR

Choking

- If your pet is choking, use your finger to sweep the back of the mouth to try to remove the blockage.

- Only do this in an unconscious patient, as there is a high risk of a bite injury.

- Avoid pushing the obstruction further down.

How to Remove an Obstruction

Heimlich Maneuver

- If your pet is still standing, wrap your arms around the abdomen just under the rib cage.

- Firmly perform 3 thrusts in succession. This can also be performed while they are on their back.

- Check if the obstruction has come up with a visual exam of the mouth.

- Finger-sweep the back of the mouth to remove the blockage if you can see it and the patient is unconscious.

- If your pet is still choking, try 5 brisk thrusts to the back between the shoulder blades.

- If this does not work and your pet is not breathing, start CPR (see p. 14) and transport to your veterinarian immediately.

Diagram 2.1. Heimlich Maneuver

External Extraction Technique (XXT)™

Only use this technique in an unconscious patient that has obstructed on a ball or similar shaped object.

0. Indications:
- ✓ Full airway obstruction AND
- ✓ Ball or similar shaped hazard AND
- ✓ Unconscious Patient*
   (*except for very passive dogs as safety dictates)

1. Starting Body Position:
   a. *"Brace the Back"* against the floor
   Straddle dog in supine position
   (adjust based on size of dog)

   b. Position head in "In-Line position"
   with airway parallel to floor
   "Nose, ears, spine, all in a line"

2. Identify Landmarks:
   a. Feel the ball:

3. Starting Hand Position:
   a. Thumbs placed:
   - both sides of trachea, caudal to (below) the ball
   - note the space between the thumbs

   b. Middle Fingers:
   pushing into the 'V' notch to help open jaw

   c. Index Fingers:
   grip using lip/cheek to protect fingers

4. PUSH HARD!!
   a. J-Stroke:
   pushing with locked out arms and full body strength,
   down and out against the ball,
   opening jaw so that ball ejects out of mouth

5. If breathing does not return spontaneously
   a. Provide 2 Mouth-to-Snout Rescue Breaths

6. If patient does not respond
   a. Begin CPR

7. Follow your VEMSPlan™
   a. Communications, Transportation, Continued Care

CPR (Cardiopulmonary Resuscitation)

Transporting your pet to the nearest veterinary facility is extremely important as soon as it's safe to do so.

ABC's: Airway, Breathing, Circulation

- CPR is done to try to restart the heart and breathing in an emergency.

- Starting blood flow back to the heart and body is imperative to do as quickly as possible.

- As soon as it is safe to do so, transport to the nearest veterinary hospital.

Airway

1. Check if your pet is breathing by observing if their chest is rising and falling.

2. Place a tissue in front of the nose and see if it moves to confirm airflow.

3. Try to arouse them by vigorously rubbing them and calling their name.

4. Examine the mouth and throat for any obstructions.

Breathing

If your pet is not breathing, follow these steps:

1. Extend the neck to align it with the spine.

2. Pull the tongue out so it helps keep the airway open.

3. Use one hand to tightly close the mouth and keep the lips sealed so no air escapes.

4. In cats and small dogs, hold the corners of the mouth closed tightly.

5. With the other hand, create a seal over the snout.

6. Blow into the nostrils twice to make the chest rise and fall.

7. You can also help stimulate respiration by pressing your nail onto the GV26 (governing vessel) acupuncture point, located between the nose and the lip. See Diagram 2.4 for the location of the GV26 point in a cat and dog.

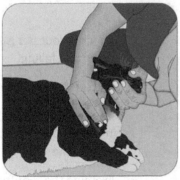

Diagram 2.3

Diagram 2.4. The red dot under the nose marks the GV26 point.

Circulation

If your pet is breathing, check for a heartbeat:

1. Locate the heart by pulling up the elbow when your pet is lying on their right side. Where the elbow meets the chest is the location of the heart.

2. Alternatively, check the femoral pulse by placing two fingers over the femoral groove

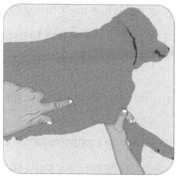

Diagram 2.5. Heart location by elbow

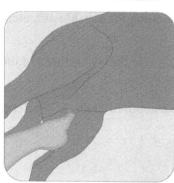

Diagram 2.6. Femoral pulse location

Steps for Chest Compressions & CPR

If your pet has both a heartbeat and is breathing, **do not** start CPR.

If there's no heartbeat, begin chest compressions:

1. Lay your pet on their right or left side (except for barrel-chested dogs).

2. Make sure they are on a hard surface like the floor or table.

3. You should be behind your pet while performing CPR.

4. Place the heel of one hand on the chest, and then place the heel of your hand on top of that hand. Lock your fingers together.

5. Lock your elbows and ensure your shoulders are directly above your hands.

6. Do not lean on the chest between compressions.

7. Follow the steps below depending on your pet's size:

For Medium to Large Dogs (Labrador, Pit bull, Mastiff, etc.): Diagram 2.7

- Compressions should be over the highest part of the chest.

- Compress the chest to a depth of 1/3 to 1/2 the chest width.

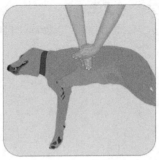

Diagram 2.7

For Barrel-chested Dogs (Bulldog, Pug, Boston Terrier, etc.): Diagram 2.8

- Lay them on their back with feet up, and compress the chest over the sternum (breastbone).

- Depress 1.5" to 4" depending on their size.

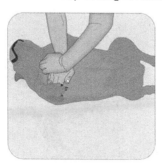

Diagram 2.8

For Dogs with Narrow (Keel) Chests (Greyhound, Whippet, etc.): Diagram 2.9

- Perform chest compressions directly over the heart using the two-handed technique.

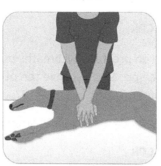

Diagram 2.9

For Cats and Small Dogs: Diagram 2.10

- Apply pressure to the chest using one or both hands, or you can compress the rib cage all the way around.

- Or perform chest compressions directly over the heart using the two-handed technique.

Diagram 2.10

For all breeds, perform chest compressions at a rate of 100–120 per minute to the beat of "Staying Alive."

Transport to the nearest veterinary hospital as soon as possible.

For Two-person CPR

- One person provides 10 breaths per minute (mouth-to-snout; see pp. 11-12), while the other person performs chest compressions.

- Check for a heartbeat every 2 minutes.

For One-person CPR

- Perform 30 chest compressions followed by 2 mouth-to-snout breaths in 2-minute cycles.

- Check for a heartbeat every 2 minutes.

Chapter 3: Normal Vital Signs

Taking the Temperature

The most accurate measure of your pet's temperature is by doing a rectal reading. To do so, follow these steps:

1. Lubricate the tip of the thermometer with petroleum jelly or water-soluble lubricant, such as K-Y jelly.

2. Lift your pet's tail and gently insert the thermometer approximately one inch into their rectum.

3. Have someone hold your pet's hind legs to prevent them from sitting or moving.

4. Wait for the thermometer to register the temperature.

5. Carefully remove the thermometer from your pet's rectum.

6. Alternatively, you can insert the end of the thermometer in between the front leg and the chest (armpit) to measure the body temperature.

Normal Temperatures

	Fahrenheit (°F)	Celsius (°C)
Dogs	101-102.5 °F	38.3-39.2 °C
Cats	100.5-102.5 °F	38.1-39.2 °C

- Hyperthermia occurs when the body temperature reaches 104 °F (40 °C) or above, and immediate cooling is required.

- Hypothermia occurs when the body temperature drops to 99 °F or below and requires warming.

Normal Heart and Respiratory Rates*

Pet Size	Resting Heart Rate (beats per minute)	Resting Respiratory Rate (breaths per minute)	Sleeping Respiratory Rate (breaths per minute)
Small (<20 lb)	100-140	15-30	10-35
Medium (20-50 lb)	70-120	15-30	10-35
Large (50-100 lb)	60-100	10-20	10-30
X-Large (>100 lb)	50-90	10-20	10-30
Cats (10+ lb)	120-180	16-40	8-20

These are general guidelines, and individual dogs and cats may have variations in their resting heart and respiratory rates.

Sleeping Respiratory Rate (SRR)

This is the respiratory rate when your pet is asleep. If elevated, it can be an indicator of congestive heart failure or other lung diseases.

Normal Blood Sugar

Normal blood sugar for both dogs and cats is 80-120 milligrams per deciliter (mg/dL).

Hydration

To assess how hydrated your pet is:

Method 1: Capillary Refill Time (CRT)

- Press your finger on the upper gums above the canine tooth. The gum should be moist.

- The gum will blanche (turn white) and should return to pink within 2 seconds.

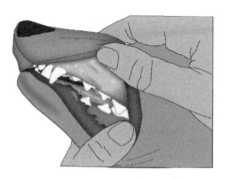

Diagram 3.1

- If the color doesn't return within 3 seconds, you should seek veterinary care.

Method 2: Skin Tent Test

- Lift the loose skin behind the head and release.

- How long it takes to return to normal will indicate if your pet is dehydrated.

- The skin will immediately go back down in a pet with normal hydration.

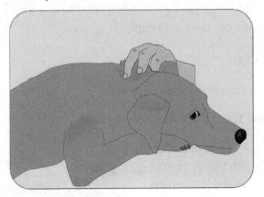

Diagram 3.2

Levels of Dehydration

Dehydration of 7% or above is a concern, and you should seek veterinary care immediately.

Dehydration Level	Capillary Refill Time (CRT)*	Skin Tent	Other Symptoms
5% - mild	<2 seconds	Skin goes back slowly	Gums semidry
7% - moderate	2-4 seconds	Skin takes a long time to go back	Gums dry Eyes sunken Lethargic Weak/fast pulse
10% - severe	>4 seconds	Skin says tented	Gums very dry Eyes sunken Very lethargic Weak heart rate

CRT less than 1 second can indicate shock, heatstroke, or other serious conditions.

Gum Color

Pink	Normal
White/Pale	Shock Anemia/bleeding Tylenol toxicity
Blue	Not breathing Smoke inhalation Tylenol toxicity
Bright Red	Carbon monoxide poisoning Heatstroke
Yellow	Liver issues
Brown	Tylenol toxicity

Any color other than pink can be an indication of a severe medical issue, and you should seek veterinary care right away.

Chapter 4: Basic First Aid

Wound Treatment

When a dog sustains a wound, the treatment depends on the severity and the specific location on the pet's body.

Here are some general steps to follow:

1. You may need to use a muzzle (see p. 2) or towel around the dog's head to prevent them from biting.

2. Gently clean the wound with water or soap to remove any dirt or debris. Trimming the hair around the wound helps keep it clean.

3. Apply pressure using a clean cloth or a gauze pad if the wound is bleeding.

4. Apply an antiseptic solution or ointment (triple antibiotic ointment like Neosporin) once the wound is clean and dry. This will help prevent infection and promote healing.

5. If the recent injury only affects the surface (not penetrating deep into the muscles and is less than 3 inches long), you can use surgical tissue glue on the wound edges:

   a. Pat the area dry with gauze.

   b. Apply a thin strip of glue to the skin edges.

   c. Press the skin edges together for 30-60 seconds until they stick together (take care not to get glue on your skin).

6. Depending on the location of the injury, you may need to cover it with a bandage or wrap. Use a nonstick pad to prevent the dressing from sticking to the wound (see p. 23).

7. Check the wound regularly to ensure it's healing correctly. If you notice any signs of infection, such as swelling, redness, pain, or discharge, contact your veterinarian.

8. If your veterinarian prescribes any medication, such as antibiotics or pain medication, follow the instructions for administering them.

If the injury occurred more than 12 hours ago, is deep, involves muscles and deeper structures, or surpasses a length of 1 inch, it is recommended to promptly seek veterinary care, as it often requires surgical intervention and antibiotics.

Bandaging 101

Bandages keep wounds clean and prevent your pet from licking and irritating the wound. It is very important that the bandage be applied correctly because if it's too tight, it can cut off the blood supply to the leg and cause serious complications and possible loss of a limb.

Bandaging a dog's leg can be tricky, but with some practice, it can become easier. Here are the steps to follow when wrapping a dog's leg:

Steps to Bandage an Injured Leg

1. Lay your pet on their side with the affected limb up.

2. Gently clean the wound with soapy water or saline to remove any debris in and around the wound.

3. Apply an antibiotic ointment to the wound—Neosporin, Mupirocin, etc.

4. Apply a nonstick pad to the wound, which is available at most pharmacies (also available in the PetVet Medic First Aid Kit).

5. Apply two pieces of white 1" tape, each about 5" long, to each side of the leg. Make sure the tape hangs down past the foot.

6. Next, wrap rolled stretch gauze around the limb, starting at the foot and leaving the toes out. Wrap up toward the body (not too tightly).

   Using the correct-sized material will help decrease the risk of damage to the limb by constriction. Too small, the rolled gauze causes constriction, and too wide can cause wrinkling that will irritate the skin (you can cut down the material if needed for a small dog).

   - 1" roll for small legs
   - 2" roll for medium legs
   - 3-4" roll for large legs

7. Use two layers of stretch gauze.

8. Fold the tape ends up onto the bandage material to secure the bandage.

9. Use an elastic bandage material (vet wrap, etc.) to cover the stretch gauze in the same way you applied the rolled gauze, being careful not to apply to tightly.

10. Use a piece of elastic bandage material or tape on the top of the bandage that contacts the fur to help prevent the dressing from slipping down.

11. Check the toes every few hours to make sure there is no swelling.

12. If you notice swelling, remove the bandage right away.

Remember that bandages should be changed regularly, typically every 1-2 days, or sooner if they become dirty or wet.

Always consult your veterinarian if you have any questions or concerns about bandaging your dog's leg.

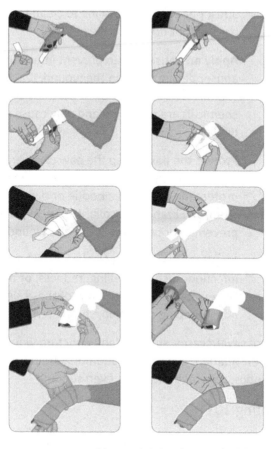

Diagram 4.1. Bandaging a dog's leg

Pad Injuries

Pad injuries in dogs can range from minor scrapes and cuts to more serious puncture wounds or burns.

Treatment will depend on the severity and extent of the damage, but here are some general steps you can take to treat a pad injury in your dog:

1. **Clean the wound:** Rinse the injured paw with lukewarm water to remove dirt or debris. You can also use a mild

antiseptic solution or saline to clean the wound. Gently pat the foot dry with a clean towel.

2. **Apply an antiseptic:** To prevent infection, use an antiseptic ointment on the wound. It is best not to use chemicals such as hydrogen peroxide or alcohol. These chemicals are too harsh and may cause a delay in healing.

3. **Protect the paw:** Keep the paw clean and dry, and limit your dog's activity to prevent further injury. You can also protect the paw with a bootie or bandage if necessary. Using an Elizabethan collar (see p. 29) is helpful to prevent your pet from licking the wound.

4. **Monitor for signs of infection:** Watch for any signs of infection, such as swelling, redness, or discharge from the wound. If you notice any of these signs, or if your dog is limping or in pain, seek veterinary attention.

In more severe cases, such as deep puncture wounds or burns, your veterinarian may suggest additional treatment, such as antibiotics, pain medication, or even surgery.

Splinting 101

Placing a splint on your pet's leg is for temporary comfort and protection until you can be seen by a veterinarian.

Muzzle your pet or use a leash (see p. 2) to help restrain your pet and keep you safe before following these steps:

1. Lay your pet on their side.

2. Cut down the splint (the PetVet Medic First Aid Kit comes with one, or you can use a rolled-up newspaper, magazine, or piece of thick cardboard) so it is larger than the bone that is affected, going past the next bone to help stabilize it. Set it aside.

3. Apply two pieces of white 1" tape, each about 5" long, to each side of the bottom of the leg. Make sure the tape hangs down past the foot.*

4. Next, wrap rolled stretch gauze around the leg, starting at the bottom and leaving the toes out. Go up toward the body, making sure to not make it too tight.

   Using the correct-sized material will help decrease the risk of damage to the limb by constriction. Too small, the rolled gauze causes constriction, and too wide can cause wrinkling that will irritate the skin (you can cut down the material if needed for a small dog).

   - 1" roll for small legs
   - 2" roll for medium legs
   - 3-4" roll for large legs

5. Use two layers of stretch gauze.

6. Fold the tape ends up onto the bandage material to secure the bandage.

7. Put the splint under the leg, making sure the open part is on top. It should cover about 50% of the leg on the back.

8. Starting at the toes again, wrap over the splint, going up the leg to just above where the bandage material ends.

9. Attach white tape along the top of the bandage and fur to help prevent it from slipping.

10. Check the toes every few hours to make sure there is no swelling.

11. Always bandage to the next joint above the fracture.

12. Use an Elizabethan collar (see p. 29) to prevent your pet from chewing the bandage or splint.

Never use duct tape on your pet's leg because this can cause serious pain when removing, can constrict the blood supply, and does not allow the skin to breathe.

Where to Place a Splint

- If the lower tibia (bone below the knee) is fractured, the splint should go just above the knee.

- If the fracture is below the elbow, the splint and bandage should finish above the elbow.

- If the toes are broken, then you splint above the next joint.

- If the upper part of a front leg (humerus) or upper part of a back leg (femur) is broken, you cannot splint those.

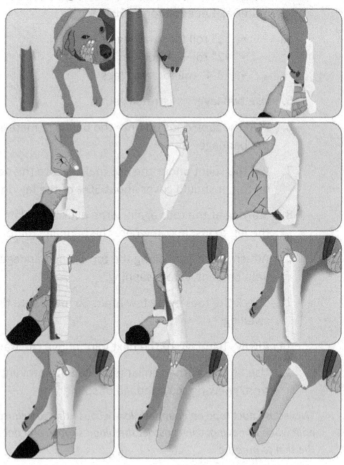

Diagram 4.2. Splinting a dog's leg

Elizabethan Collar

Elizabethan collars are a great way to help prevent your dog from licking a wound or chewing on a bandage or splint. Purchasing a pre-made plastic e-collar or blow-up comfort collar is ideal, but you can make one if necessary, using these pointers:

- **Size and fit:** Fold a towel longways to the appropriate size for your dog's neck. Wrap the towel around the dog's neck, making sure to leave the ears out. It should be snug but not too tight, allowing your dog to breathe comfortably. You should be able to put 1 finger between the towel and your pet's neck.

- **Material choice:** Pick a sturdy towel that is not easily torn or shredded. Avoid towels with loose threads or frayed edges that could be a choking hazard.

- **Securing the towel:** Use a reliable and secure method to attach the ends of the towel. While duct tape may work in some cases, it's important to ensure it doesn't stick directly to your dog's fur, which could cause discomfort or skin irritation. Consider using safety pins or strong clips that won't harm your dog.

- **Supervision:** Keep a close eye on your dog while they wear the towel collar to ensure they don't accidentally injure themselves or remove the collar. If you notice any signs of distress or discomfort, it's best to remove the makeshift collar and consult a veterinarian for alternative options.

Diagram 4.3

Bleeding

Bleeding can occur from trauma (bite wounds, being hit by a car, etc.), certain poisons, clotting disorders, and infections. Here's how you can stop the bleeding:

1. **Restrain your dog:** If your dog is bleeding heavily, keeping them calm and still is important. Restrain your dog by placing them on a table or the ground and holding them in place.

2. **Muzzle your pet:** Some dogs will bite when they are in pain.

3. **Locate the wound:** Once your dog is restrained, try to locate the source of the bleeding. Gently remove any debris or foreign objects that may be in the injury.

4. **Apply pressure:** Using a clean cloth or gauze, apply firm pressure to the wound for several minutes to help stop the bleeding. If the material becomes soaked with blood, do not remove it; apply more cloth on top.

5. **Elevate the wound:** If possible, elevate the wound above the level of the heart to help slow down the bleeding.

6. **Seek veterinary care:** Even if the bleeding seems to stop, it's important to take your dog to a veterinarian as soon as possible for further evaluation and treatment. In some cases, internal bleeding or other complications may occur.

7. **Cover the wound:** Before transporting your dog, cover the wound with a clean cloth or gauze to help prevent further contamination and bleeding.

Bleeding Toenail

This commonly occurs when trimming a dog's nails, especially when they have dark nails, which makes it difficult to see the nail quicks.

Treatment

1. Apply pressure to the end of the nail that is bleeding.

2. Place Kwik Stop styptic powder on the tip of the nail, and hold pressure for a few minutes.

3. If Kwik Stop or similar stop-bleeding powder isn't available, you can try applying cornstarch or flour at home. Apply to the end of the quick with pressure for a few minutes, then release.

4. In the unlikely event that the nail continues to bleed, then you should be seen by your veterinarian.

Chapter 5: Heatstroke, Hypothermia, and Hypoglycemia

Heatstroke (Hyperthermia)

Heatstroke occurs when your pet's body temperature is 104 °F or higher.

Causes

- Breeds that are brachycephalic (have short noses)

  Brachycephalic pets, such as pugs and bulldogs, have narrow air passages and often excessive tissue around the back of the mouth. This leads to breathing difficulties further aggravated by heat, which can cause swelling.

- Excessive heat, such as leaving your pet inside a car with the windows closed or outside on a hot day

- Infection

- Toxins

- Seizures

Symptoms

Panting/trouble breathing	Red or glassy eyes	Warm ears or nose
Loss of appetite	Runny nose	Lethargy
Shivering	Coughing	Vomiting

Treatment

1. Remove your pet from the hot environment immediately.

2. Lay towels soaked in cold water over your pet. *Be careful not to cool them down too quickly.*

3. Wrap a thin towel around an icepack or small bag of ice and place under the armpits.

4. Make sure there is cold water for your pet available to drink (add ice to water if possible).

5. Transport immediately to an emergency clinic for treatment if the temperature is greater than 104 °F or they have difficulty breathing.

6. Never leave your pet in a parked car. Diagram 5.1 shows how quickly the temperature can spike.

Diagram 5.1

Hypothermia (Low Body Temperature)

Hypothermia occurs when your pet's body temperature drops below 99 °F.

Symptoms

Early Signs	Late Signs
Lethargy/confusion	Collapse
Shivering	Lack of shivering
Stiffness	Pupils fixed & dilated
Ataxia/difficulty walking	Slow breathing & heartbeat
Pale gums	Comatose
Cold to the touch	Death possible

Treatment

1. Remove your pet from the cold if possible.

2. Wrap them in warm towels and/or blankets (use a dryer to warm up towels and blankets).

3. Use a heating pad. Place a towel between your pet and the heating pad so it's not in direct contact with the skin.

4. Transport to the nearest veterinary clinic for treatment.

Hypoglycemia (Low Blood Sugar)

Normal blood sugar level for dogs should be 68-104 mg/dL. For cats, it should be 71-182 mg/dL. Hypoglycemia is anything less than 60.

Causes

- Overdose of insulin
- Nursing animals
- Infection
- Seizures
- Small breed puppies not getting enough calories
- Liver shunts
- Xylitol toxicity (see p. 54)
- Parasites and other medical conditions

Symptoms

Tremors	Lethargy	Seizures
Loss of balance	Vomiting	Diarrhea

If you suspect your pet has low blood sugar, it is important to seek veterinary care as soon as possible. Your vet can perform blood tests to confirm the diagnosis and provide appropriate treatment.

In the meantime, there are some things you can do at home to help manage low blood sugar:

For Young Puppies and Kittens

- **Encourage nursing:** Make sure the puppies or kittens are nursing regularly and getting enough milk. You may need to help position the puppies properly and ensure they latch on correctly.

- **Supplement with formula:** If the puppies are not getting enough milk from their mother, you may need to supplement with a milk replacement puppy formula. *Cow's and goat's milk are not recommended because they are high in lactose and low in proteins and fat, which can lead to diarrhea and other complications.*

- Keep your nursing dog and her puppies in a warm, quiet, and stress-free environment to help them conserve energy and stay calm.

For Older Puppies/Kittens and Adult Pets

Small dog breeds, such as Yorkshire terrier, Chihuahua, toy poodle, Maltese, and Pomeranian, are at a higher risk of developing low blood sugar because of their size.

- If your dog can sit up and swallow, you can attempt to give them some sugar mixed with a little water, or you can smear Karo syrup on the gums. Only use a small amount at a time to make sure they are swallowing and not aspirating it into their lungs.

- Offer small, frequent meals throughout the day. You can moisten kibble with water to entice eating.

- Nutri-Cal can be purchased from most pet stores or online and is a good supplement to give small-breed dogs to maintain their blood sugar.

- Provide high-fat meals like puppy food.

For Nursing Mothers

- If your nursing dog or cat is showing signs of low blood sugar, the puppies or kittens should be immediately removed from the mother and supplemented with an appropriate milk replacement formula, such as Esbilac.

- Offer the mother small, frequent meals throughout the day.

- Switching her to puppy food during the pregnancy and while she is nursing helps maintain her high-caloric requirement. Alternatively, adding boiled chicken or cottage cheese to the food may help encourage her to eat more.

- Nursing mothers can also be deficient in calcium. Tums can be given in dosages of 25-50mg/kg per day for oral calcium (see dosing chart on p. 140).

Overall, working closely with your veterinarian to manage low blood sugar is important. With prompt and appropriate treatment, most pets recover fully from hypoglycemia.

Chapter 6: Toxic Plants, Algae, and Mushrooms

Pets, particularly dogs and cats, are naturally curious and love to explore their surroundings. Unfortunately, their curiosity can sometimes lead them into danger, especially when it comes to various plants, fungi, and algae. Many common houseplants, outdoor plants, mushrooms, and algae can be toxic to pets, causing symptoms ranging from mild irritation to severe illness and even death.

This chapter will cover the top 13 toxic plants, fungi, and algae for pets, along with photos to help you identify these hazards and keep them safely out of reach.

Aloe Vera

Gel and sap inside the plant can be toxic to pets, particularly cats.

Ingesting aloe vera can cause vomiting, diarrhea, lethargy, and a loss of appetite.

Avoid using aloe vera products on your pets, such as lotions and shampoos.

Autumn Crocus

Ingesting any part of the plant is toxic. Severe gastrointestinal symptoms, organ damage, and bone marrow suppression can occur in dogs and cats.

Azaleas & Rhododendron

Toxic to pets, particularly dogs.

All plant parts, including the leaves, flowers, and stems, are toxic.

Ingesting even a small amount of these substances can cause vomiting, diarrhea, drooling, difficulty breathing, and irregular heartbeat.

Blue-Green Algae (Cyanobacteria)

- It's common in lakes and ponds (standing water), especially in warm climates, and appears as a green or blue murky layer on top of the water.

- It's not actually algae; it's a type of bacteria that can be toxic to animals AND humans.

Symptoms

Symptoms can occur within 15 minutes or several days after exposure.

Vomiting	Difficulty walking	Diarrhea	Breathing difficulty
Weakness	Seizures	Drooling	Pale gums
Liver failure	Kidney failure	Death possible	

Treatment

- Rinse your dog's mouth and body immediately with clean water if you think they were exposed to contaminated water, and monitor for symptoms.

- Seek veterinary care immediately.

Castor Bean

The seeds contain ricin, a highly toxic substance. It affects the gastrointestinal system, kidneys, and liver in dogs and cats.

Dieffenbachia (Dumb Cane)

It contains calcium oxalate crystals and causes oral irritation, excessive drooling, and difficulty swallowing in pets.

English Ivy

Ivy is toxic to dogs and cats and causes gastrointestinal upset, such as vomiting and diarrhea. Skin contact may also cause irritation.

Holly

It can cause nausea, severe vomiting, and diarrhea.

Lilies

Mainly toxic to cats, but dogs can be affected.

Many varieties of lilies, including Easter lilies, tiger lilies, and daylilies, are toxic.

Even ingesting a small amount can cause kidney failure and other severe symptoms, including vomiting, lethargy, and loss of appetite.

Marijuana (THC)

It can cause depression or lethargy, lack of coordination, dilated pupils, drooling, vomiting, urinary incontinence (dribbling urine), low body temperature, slow heart, and

slow respiratory rate. In severe cases, pets may have muscle tremors or seizures.

Mistletoe

Heart problems, difficulty breathing, and gastrointestinal upset can occur.

Mushrooms

Poisonous mushrooms can be very dangerous for pets if ingested and can cause a range of symptoms, from mild gastrointestinal upset to severe organ damage or even death. Dogs, cats, and other animals may be attracted to mushrooms in the yard or on walks and can accidentally consume poisonous varieties.

There are many types of poisonous mushrooms, but some of the most dangerous for pets include:

Amanita Mushrooms

These can cause severe liver damage and even death in dogs and cats.

Death Cap Mushrooms

Death caps are highly toxic and can cause liver and kidney damage as well as seizures and death in dogs and cats.

False Morel Mushrooms

These can cause vomiting, diarrhea, and even seizures in dogs and cats.

Symptoms

Symptoms of mushroom toxicity in pets can vary depending on the type of mushroom ingested and the amount consumed but may include:

Photo courtesy Wikipedia

Vomiting	Diarrhea	Painful abdomen
Drooling	Lethargy	Weakness
Lack of coordination	Seizures	Jaundice (yellowing of eyes/skin)

If you suspect that your pet has ingested a poisonous mushroom, it's important to seek veterinary care right away.

Treatment may include supportive care, such as IV fluids and medications to manage symptoms, and monitoring of liver and kidney function.

In cases where you cannot access emergency care within 2 hours (and your pet is not showing any symptoms), you can induce vomiting with 3% hydrogen peroxide (see p. 148).

To prevent mushroom toxicity in pets, check the yard and other outdoor areas for mushrooms and remove them promptly. Avoid letting your pets roam in areas where mushrooms are known to grow, and keep them on a leash during walks to prevent accidental ingestion. If you're unsure whether a mushroom is safe for your pet to eat, it's best to err on the side of caution and avoid it altogether.

Oleander

All parts of the plant are toxic. Severe symptoms can occur, including cardiac abnormalities, vomiting, and tremors.

Sago Palm

Dogs are particularly susceptible.

All plant parts, including the leaves, stem, and seeds, contain a toxic substance called cycasin.

Ingesting even a small amount of cycasin can cause severe liver failure and other symptoms, including vomiting, diarrhea, abdominal pain, lethargy, and seizures.

Tulips & Hyacinths

Toxic to pets, particularly dogs.

Bulbs are the most toxic, but other parts can be as well.

Ingesting even a small amount of these substances can cause vomiting, diarrhea, drooling, and difficulty breathing.

Note that this is not an exhaustive list, and many other plants, fungi, and algae can be toxic to pets. As a responsible pet owner, you should research the plants, mushrooms, and algae you bring into your home, garden, or any areas your pets frequent to ensure they are safe for your furry friends. If you suspect your pet has ingested a toxic substance, seek veterinary care immediately.

For a more extensive list of plants, fungi, and algae that are toxic to pets, visit the ASPCA website: https://www.aspca.org/pet-care/animal-poison-control.

Chapter 7: Food Toxicities

Alcohol

Alcohol is toxic to both dogs and cats. Even a small amount of alcohol can cause severe problems and sometimes be fatal.

Products containing alcohol include alcoholic drinks, high-level sanitizers, mouthwash, rising bread, certain antifreeze, and cleaning products.

Symptoms

Vomiting	Thirst	Lethargy	Loss of balance
Blindness	Tremors	Coma	Seizures

Treatment

Seek veterinary care immediately.

Chocolate

Chocolate contains methylxanthines, which are primarily theobromine and caffeine, and are very toxic to animals.

- Theobromine and caffeine produce similar effects, but the effects of theobromine last much longer.

- Baking chocolate has the highest levels of theobromine, which makes it the most toxic for pets. Semisweet is the next most toxic followed by dark chocolate, milk chocolate, and chocolate-flavored cakes or cookies.

- White chocolate has very low levels of theobromine and rarely causes issues other than an upset stomach.

Symptoms

Symptoms are typically seen within 2 hours.

Vomiting	Diarrhea	Hyperactivity	Tremors
Seizures	Racing heart rate	Abnormal heart rhythm	Death possible

Treatment

- If the chocolate was ingested within 2 hours (and your dog is not showing symptoms), you can induce vomiting (see p. 148).
- If your pet is already showing symptoms, they should be transported to a veterinary clinic immediately.

Toxin binders like charcoal are helpful. It is recommended to feed a bland diet for 2-3 days to settle the stomach in mild cases (see p. 97).

Chocolate Calculator

Scan the QR code below or go to www.petvetproduct.com/pages/chocolate-toxicity-calculator for a chocolate calculator that can calculate the approximate toxic dose:

Please double check that the calculated results are appropriate (i.e., "in the ballpark"), and use these at your own risk. Pets with certain health conditions like heart, kidney, and liver disease may have lower thresholds for chocolate toxicity.

Coffee

Coffee ingestion can be harmful to dogs and cats due to the presence of caffeine, which is a central nervous system stimulant.

Symptoms

Restlessness	Agitation	Rapid breathing	Heart palpitations
Tremors	Seizures	Death possible	

The severity of symptoms depends on the amount of caffeine ingested and the pet's size. Small pets are more susceptible to the toxic effects of caffeine than larger pets. Generally, a dose of 150 mg/kg of caffeine can be lethal to pets.

Note that other sources of caffeine, such as tea, chocolate, energy drinks, and some medications, can also be harmful to pets. It's best to keep all caffeine-containing products out of reach of pets.

Treatment

Transport your pet to a veterinarian immediately if you suspect your pet has ingested caffeine or any other toxic substance.

Grapes & Raisins

Grapes and raisins can be toxic to pets and can lead to kidney failure in some animals, especially those with underlying medical conditions. Dogs are much more likely to ingest grapes and raisins than cats, but they're toxic to both.

Symptoms

Signs usually begin within several hours of ingestion. Vomiting almost always occurs, and grapes can be seen in the vomit. Other symptoms are:

Diarrhea	Not eating	Dehydration
Painful stomach	Drooling	Lethargy

Within 1-5 days after ingestion, you may notice:

Excessive drinking	Excessive urination	Weakness
Swelling of legs	Trembling	Loss of balance

The toxic dose can vary depending on the individual animal. The following charts give a general idea of the potential toxicity based on weight.

Note that even small amounts of grapes and raisins can be toxic to dogs and cats. It's crucial to seek veterinary attention immediately if you suspect your pet has ingested grapes or raisins.

Grape Toxicity Chart

Note that a toxic dose is 0.7 oz/kg.

Dog's Weight	Toxic Amount in Ounces (0.7 oz/kg)	Number of Grapes That Are Toxic*
5 lb	1.5 oz	6-9 grapes
10 lb	3.2 oz	12-19 grapes
15 lb	4.8 oz	19-28 grapes

20 lb	6.4 oz	25-38 grapes
25 lb	8 oz	32-48 grapes
30 lb	9.5 oz	38-57 grapes
35 lb	11 oz	44-66 grapes
40 lb	12.7 oz	50-76 grapes
45 lb	14 oz	56-84 grapes
50 lb	15.9 oz	63-95 grapes
55 lb	17.5 oz	70-105 grapes
60 lb	19 oz	76-114 grapes

Raisin Toxicity Chart

A toxic dose of raisins is 0.11 oz/kg.

Dog's Weight	Toxic Amount in Ounces (0.11 oz/kg)	Approx. Number of Raisins That Are Toxic*
5 lb	0.25 oz	15 raisins
10 lb	0.5 oz	30 raisins
15 lb	0.75 oz	45 raisins
20 lb	1 oz	60 raisins
25 lb	1.25 oz	75 raisins
30 lb	1.5 oz	90 raisins
35 lb	1.75 oz	105 raisins
40 lb	2 oz	120 raisins

45 lb	2.25 oz	135 raisins
50 lb	2.5 oz	150 raisins
55 lb	2.75 oz	165 raisins
60 lb	3 oz	180 raisins

Please note that the size of grapes and raisins can vary depending on their type, so the charts provided are an approximate estimate of the average size of a grape and raisin (4-6 grapes per oz and 60 raisins per oz).

Treatment

- If your dog has ingested a toxic dose of grapes or raisins within the last 1-2 hours, you can try to induce vomiting (see p. 148) to remove most of the grapes. DO NOT INDUCE VOMITING IN A CAT.

- If you cannot do this or are uncomfortable, then take your pet immediately to your veterinarian.

- If your pet is already showing symptoms of grape or raisin toxicity, please take your pet to the nearest veterinarian for treatment. Treatment may include medications to help decrease absorption of the toxin, IV fluids, and other medications.

Macadamia Nuts

Symptoms

Symptoms usually start within 12 hours.

Weakness	Hyperthermia (overheating)	Lethargy	Tremors
Vomiting	Loss of balance	Depression	

Treatment

- Induce vomiting (see p. 148) if ingestion is within 2 hours and they are not showing any symptoms.

- Give activated charcoal (see p. 145).

- Transport to your local veterinarian.

- The prognosis is good with early decontamination and supportive care.

Moldy Food or Nuts

Moldy food, especially nuts, can contain tremorgenic mycotoxins, which cause tremors.

Symptoms

Muscle tremors	Loss of balance	Seizures

Treatment

- If your pet ingested moldy food within the last hour, you can try inducing vomiting (see p. 148). Do not attempt if showing symptoms already.

- Seek veterinary care.

Onions/Garlic/Chives (Allium)

All forms can be toxic—fresh, cooked, and dehydrated (like in soups, baby food, etc.).

Cats are more susceptible, but dogs are also at risk.

Symptoms

Weakness	Pale or blue gums
Red urine	Exercise intolerance
Anemia	

Treatment

- **Dogs:** If onion is ingested within 2 hours, you can induce vomiting with hydrogen peroxide (see p. 148).

- **Cats:** DO NOT INDUCE VOMITING—transfer to your veterinarian immediately.

Rising Bread Dough

- Ingesting rising bread dough is potentially life-threatening if not treated right away.

- Ethanol/alcohol is produced from the dough as it rises.

- Body heat causes the dough to rise further and can lead to a foreign-body obstruction.

Symptoms

Pain	Bloating	Vomiting
Lethargy	Loss of balance	

Treatment

- Induce vomiting (see p. 148) if you know your dog ingested the bread dough within 30 minutes, AND the dog is not showing any symptoms (do not induce vomiting if your pet is already showing symptoms).

- If the dough doesn't come up or it's been longer than 30 minutes, transport them to your nearest veterinarian.

Xylitol (Birch Sugar)

Xylitol, also known as birch sugar, is a sugar substitute commonly found in sugar-free products, especially chewing gum, some peanut butters, sugar-free jams and syrups, Tic Tac mints, and Mentos mints. While xylitol is safe for human consumption, it can be highly toxic to dogs because it increases their insulin, which causes a drop in blood sugar (hypoglycemia) and can cause liver failure. Xylitol may not be as toxic to cats, but it's still best to avoid giving xylitol to them.

Symptoms

Vomiting	Weakness	Difficulty walking/standing
Tremors	Seizures	Liver failure
Coma	Death possible	

Treatment

- If you suspect your dog has ingested xylitol, acting quickly is important.

- If ingestion just occurred, you can feed your dog some bread and then induce vomiting with hydrogen peroxide (see p. 148).

- However, if you're uncomfortable doing this or your dog is already showing symptoms of xylitol poisoning, it's crucial to seek veterinary care immediately.

Chapter 8: Emergency Situations

Bloat (GDV: Gastric Dilatation-Volvulus)

GDV develops when a dog's stomach becomes filled with gas. The stomach twists on itself, leading to a blockage of blood flow to the stomach and spleen.

It can cause significant damage to the organs and can be life-threatening.

Causes

1. **Eating too quickly:** Dogs that eat their meals too fast or gulp their food are more likely to swallow air, which can cause the stomach to distend and twist.

2. **Exercise after eating:** Exercising vigorously right after a meal can increase the risk of bloat, particularly in larger breeds. It is recommended to wait at least 1-2 hours before exercising.

3. **Genetics:** Certain breeds such as basset hound, Doberman pinscher, Gordon setter, Great Dane, Irish setter, Old English sheepdog, Saint Bernard, standard poodle, and Weimaraner are more predisposed to bloat than others due to their anatomical structure. But it can occur in any breed or size.

4. **Stress:** Stressful situations, such as travel or a change in routine, can increase the likelihood of bloat in some dogs.

5. **Age:** Older dogs may be more susceptible to bloat than younger dogs.

6. **Gender:** Male dogs are more likely to develop bloat than females.

Symptoms

Distended abdomen	Drooling	Retching (trying to vomit)
Panting	Restlessness	Pain

It's essential to be aware of the risk factors associated with bloat and take steps to reduce the likelihood of this potentially life-threatening condition. You can use a special feeder (slow feeder) to slow their eating, and you should avoid exercising your dog right after a meal.

Treatment

- Transport your dog to the nearest veterinarian or emergency clinic as soon as possible.

- Without prompt intervention, the prognosis is poor.

- In breeds prone to bloating, a preventive surgery can be done to tack the stomach down to decrease the risk of it twisting and causing bloat.

Bone Ingestion

Symptoms

Obstruction	Ulceration
Constipation	Damage to digestive tract

Chicken Bones

- Do not induce vomiting.

- Start a bland diet (see p. 97) and consult your veterinarian.

- If your pet is vomiting, acting lethargic, or not eating, you should consult your veterinarian right away.

Large Bones, Ham Bones, or Ribs

- Do not induce vomiting.

- Consult your veterinarian.

It's recommended to avoid giving bones to dogs to prevent potential complications.

Burns

Treating burns in pets depends on the severity and extent of the burn. Seek veterinary care immediately if your pet has suffered a burn. Here are some general steps you can take to help your pet until you can get them to a veterinarian:

1. **Remove your pet from the source of the burn:** If the burn was caused by a heat source, such as a stove or fireplace, or a chemical, such as cleaning agents or gasoline, remove your pet from the source immediately.

2. **Flush the area with water:** Use cool water to flush the affected area for several minutes. This will help cool the burn and remove any chemical residue.

3. **Cover the burn:** Apply burn cream (silver wound gel), which you can buy over the counter at most drug stores. Cover the burn with a sterile, non-adhesive bandage to help prevent infection.

4. **Provide pain relief:** If your pet is in pain, you can provide over-the-counter pain relief medication such as aspirin, but only under the guidance of a veterinarian.

5. **Seek veterinary care:** Burns can be very painful and can quickly become infected, so seek veterinary care as soon as possible. Your veterinarian may prescribe pain relief medication along with antibiotics to prevent infection and

may recommend wound care or other treatment, depending on the severity of the burn.

Note that some burns, especially those caused by chemicals or electrical sources, can be very serious and may require emergency care.

Carbon Monoxide (CO) Poisoning

Carbon monoxide is an odorless and colorless toxic gas, which makes it very dangerous because it's difficult to detect.

Common Sources

- Heaters

- Appliances

- Smoke

- Running cars

- Running boats

Symptoms

Coughing/ gagging	Trouble breathing	Elevated heart rate
Drooling	Vomiting	Loss of balance
Seizures	Coma	Death possible

Treatment

- Remove your pet from the source of CO immediately if safe to do so.

- Transport your pet to your veterinarian immediately.

- Oxygen is one of the main treatments for CO poisoning. Your veterinarian may also administer fluids and other medications to help your pet.

Diabetic Ketoacidosis (DKA)

Diabetic ketoacidosis occurs when a diabetic dog has a deficiency in insulin. This can lead to prolonged blood sugar, which can cause electrolyte abnormalities and high levels of ketones. This is potentially life-threatening without prompt and appropriate treatment.

Symptoms

Drinking excessively	Urinating excessively	Decreased appetite
Vomiting	Diarrhea	Weight loss
Lethargy	Liver issues	

Treatment

- Your pet should be seen immediately by a veterinarian.

- Hospitalization with IV fluids, insulin, and electrolyte therapy are some of the treatments your pet will need.

Drowning

If you suspect your pet is drowning, it is important to act quickly to help them. Here are the steps you should take:

1. **Get your pet out of the water:** If possible, pull your pet out of the water as soon as you can. Be careful not to get injured yourself.

2. **Check their breathing:** Check to see if your pet is breathing. If they are not breathing, start CPR immediately (see p. 14).

3. **Keep your pet warm:** Wrap them in a warm blanket or towel to help them maintain their body temperature.

4. **Seek veterinary care:** Even if your pet seems fine, take them to a veterinarian as soon as possible. Your veterinarian can check for any signs of injury or damage and monitor your pet for potential complications.

Remember, prevention is the best way to protect your pet from drowning. Always supervise your pet around water, and consider using a life jacket if your pet will be swimming in open water.

Electric Shock

Electric shock in dogs and cats can result in a range of symptoms, from mild to severe.

Symptoms

Burns on skin or in the mouth	Difficulty breathing	Irregular heartbeat
Muscle tremors	Seizures	Loss of consciousness

If you suspect that your pet has been electrocuted, it is important to take immediate action. Here are some steps to take:

1. **Turn off the power source:** If your pet is still in contact with the source of the electricity, turn off the power source immediately if safe to do so.

2. **Check for breathing and a heartbeat:** If your pet is not breathing or has no heartbeat, begin CPR (see p. 14) and seek veterinary attention as soon as possible.

3. **Move your pet to safety:** If your pet is conscious and breathing, move them to a safe area away from the source of the electricity.

4. **Check for burns:** Look for any signs of burns on your pet's skin or mouth. If you see any burns, seek veterinary attention immediately.

5. **Transport to your veterinarian:** Seek veterinary attention immediately if your pet has been electrocuted, even if they seem to be acting normally. Electric shock can cause internal damage and heart/lung issues that may not be immediately apparent, and prompt treatment can improve your pet's chances of full recovery.

Fractures

If you suspect your dog has fractured a leg or their back, handle them with extreme care. It's advisable to use a muzzle (see p. 2), because dogs in pain may bite, even their owners.

The PetVet Medic First Aid Kit includes a splint that can be trimmed to fit your dog or cat. If your pet's leg is unstable or appears to be hanging abnormally, you can apply a temporary splint to provide support until a veterinarian is able to assess the injury (see p. 26).

Gunshot

Gunshots can cause serious damage, and your pet should be seen right away by your veterinarian.

Here are some steps you can take while transporting your pet to the veterinary hospital:

1. Keep your pet as calm and still as possible. This may mean gently restraining or wrapping them in a towel or blanket to prevent further injury. You may need to muzzle them to prevent a bite (see p. 2).

2. Apply direct pressure to the wound using a clean cloth or bandage to help slow or stop bleeding.

3. Do not attempt to remove the bullet or any objects from the wound because this can cause further damage.

4. If your pet is unconscious or not breathing, perform CPR (see p. 14).

Once you arrive at the veterinary hospital, the veterinarian will evaluate your pet's condition and determine the best course of treatment, which may include surgery, antibiotics, and pain medication.

Head Injury

Head trauma in dogs can be a serious condition and requires immediate medical attention.

Symptoms

- **Loss of consciousness or altered mental state:** Dogs with head trauma may lose consciousness or show signs of confusion, disorientation, or altered behavior.

- **Seizures:** Seizures can be a sign of a serious head injury and may occur immediately after the injury or days later.

- **Abnormal eye movements:** Dogs with head trauma may show abnormal eye movements, such as rapid eye movements (nystagmus) or unequal pupils.

- **Difficulty walking or standing:** Head trauma can affect a dog's coordination, causing them to stumble, fall, or have difficulty standing.

- **Abnormal breathing:** Dogs with head trauma may have trouble breathing or display irregular breathing patterns.

- **Bleeding from the nose or ears:** If the head trauma is severe, bleeding from the nose or ears may occur.

- **Vomiting or nausea:** Head trauma can cause dogs to experience vomiting, nausea, or loss of appetite.

If you suspect your dog has sustained head trauma, it's important to seek veterinary care immediately.

Treatment

Treatment may include diagnostic testing, such as imaging studies or blood tests, as well as medication, surgery, or supportive care, depending on the severity of the injury.

Heart Disease

Congestive heart failure (CHF) is a serious medical condition that can affect dogs and cats, particularly those in their senior years. It happens when the heart is unable to efficiently pump blood, leading to the accumulation of fluid in the lungs and other tissues.

Symptoms

Symptoms depend on the severity of the condition.

Lethargy	Difficulty breathing	Coughing
Pale or blue gums	Loss of appetite	Weight loss
Fainting or collapse	Swollen abdomen	Sleeping respiratory rate >30

CHF is a medical emergency—transport to your nearest veterinary hospital.

1. **Diagnosis:** Your veterinarian will perform a thorough physical examination, blood tests, chest X-rays, and an electrocardiogram to diagnose CHF. Additional tests, such as an echocardiogram or cardiac ultrasound, may also be necessary to determine the underlying cause of CHF.

2. **Treatment:** Treatment for CHF may include medications such as diuretics, ACE inhibitors, beta-blockers, and vasodilators to help improve heart function, reduce fluid buildup, and improve blood flow. Oxygen therapy may also be necessary in severe cases. Your veterinarian will develop a treatment plan tailored to your pet's needs.

3. **Management:** CHF is a chronic condition that requires ongoing management and monitoring. This may include regular check-ups with your veterinarian, medications, dietary changes, and exercise restrictions. Your veterinarian may also recommend regularly monitoring your pet's blood pressure, heart rate, and sleeping respiratory rate (see p. 18).

4. **Prognosis:** The prognosis for CHF depends on the underlying cause and the severity of the condition. With appropriate treatment and management, many pets with CHF can enjoy a good quality of life for months or even years. However, CHF is progressive, and the prognosis can vary from pet to pet.

It's important to work closely with your veterinarian to develop a treatment plan that meets your pet's needs and to monitor them closely for signs of worsening or improvement. Early diagnosis and treatment can help improve your pet's quality of life and lifespan.

Hit by Car (HBC)

Dogs are notorious for getting out of yards and going on their own field trips. Unfortunately, sometimes they get themselves into trouble and can be hit by a car.

- Being hit by a car can cause fractures, collapsed lung, internal bleeding, and head trauma.

- Take your pet to the nearest veterinary clinic for an examination to ensure there are no life-threatening issues.

- If your pet is not breathing or their heart stops, you should start CPR (see p. 14).

Respiratory Distress

Difficulty breathing can be due to various underlying causes, such as trauma, heart disease, pneumonia, asthma, and bleeding. Heart disease can cause fluid to accumulate in the lungs, which is called pulmonary edema. It is important to recognize the signs of respiratory distress early and seek immediate veterinary care, because it can quickly progress to life-threatening conditions.

Symptoms

Shallow breathing	Wheezing/ coughing	Restlessness/ Anxiety
Weakness or lethargy	Bluish gums or tongue	Labored breathing/ panting

Treatment

Treatment for respiratory distress depends on the underlying cause and may involve:

- Diagnostic tests such as blood work, X-rays, and ultrasound

- Medications like bronchodilators, antibiotics, or steroids

- Oxygen therapy or surgery in some cases

This is a critical emergency, and you should safely transport your pet to the nearest emergency clinic.

Seizures

A seizure is a sudden and uncontrolled burst of electrical activity in the brain, which can cause a wide range of symptoms depending on the severity and location of the seizure in the brain.

Symptoms

Convulsions	Loss of consciousness	Drooling
Staring	Limb twitching	Not responsive

Causes

- Seizures can be caused by many factors, including brain tumors, infections, metabolic imbalances, toxins, low blood sugar, or genetic predisposition.

- To diagnose a seizure disorder, your veterinarian may perform a series of tests, including blood tests, imaging studies, and neurological exams.

Treatment

- Make sure your pet is on the floor and not around anything that could hurt them.

- **Vagal nerve stimulation:** Being careful not to get bitten, gently hold your pet's head and close the eyelids. Then, gently but firmly apply pressure to the eyes against the upper eyelid. You can apply pressure to one or both eyes for 10-60 seconds at a time. It can be repeated every 5 minutes if needed.

- **Massage:** You can aggressively massage the base of the dog's ears to stop or slow down a seizure.

- **Sugar solution:** Sometimes seizures are caused by low blood sugar. Nursing mothers and small breed dogs can be given a sugar solution (sugar mixed with water in a paste or Karo syrup), which can be applied to the gums. Only try this once the seizure has stopped so your pet can swallow and won't choke.

If you suspect your pet has a seizure, it's important to seek veterinary care immediately to determine the underlying cause and provide appropriate treatment. Treatment for seizures in pets may include medication, such as anticonvulsants, or changes in diet or lifestyle.

Smoke Inhalation

Smoke inhalation in dogs and cats can be a serious and potentially life-threatening condition.

- It most often occurs in a burning car or house.

- Smoke can cause lung injury and skin burns.

- Some of the by-products of smoke are carbon monoxide and cyanide, which can be life-threatening.

Symptoms

Coughing/ wheezing	Difficulty breathing	Blue or bright red gums
Rapid heartbeat	Weakness/collapse	Burns or soot around mouth/feet

Treatment

1. If safe to do so, move your pet to a safe, well-ventilated area.

2. Check your pet's breathing and pulse. If they are not breathing or their heart has stopped, start CPR immediately (see p. 14).

Smoke inhalation can cause serious lung and skin damage. Swelling in the airways can take up to 3 days to manifest, so that is why it's important to have your pet evaluated by a veterinarian as soon as possible.

Spinal Injury

Causes

- Trauma
- Breed-related malformations
- Infection
- Cancer

Symptoms

Pain in neck or back	Abnormal posture or gait	Dragging back legs
Whining	Difficulty standing or walking	Loss of bladder or bowel control

Though all dogs can have spine issues, the most common breeds affected include:

- Dachshund
- Bulldog
- Corgi
- Basset hound

Treatment

If you suspect your pet has a spinal injury, it's important to seek veterinary care right away. Waiting can cause more complications and can lead to permanent paralysis.

Avoid moving your pet as much as possible, and keep them as still and calm as you can. Your veterinarian may recommend X-rays or other diagnostic tests to assess the extent of the injury and determine the best course of treatment.

Treatment options for spinal injury can vary depending on the severity of the injury and the affected area of the spine. Conservative treatment, such as rest and pain/anti-inflammatory medication, may be recommended in some cases. More severe injuries may require surgery, physical therapy, or other interventions to help your pet recover as fully as possible.

Intervertebral Disc Disease (IVDD)

The spine consists of bony vertebrae with rubbery discs in between that act as shock absorbers. Trauma or genetics can make a disc to push up around the spinal cord and cause pressure, which can lead to permanent paralysis.

Certain breeds are at higher risk for this condition, like dachshunds with their long backs and very little support in between their front and back legs. Other breeds prone to IVDD are beagle, Doberman pinscher, cocker spaniel, French bulldog, German shepherd, Jack Russell terrier, Pekingese, Pembroke Welsh corgi, pug, shih tzu, and large breed dogs.

Symptoms

Pain	Weakness	Incontinence
Lameness	Paralysis	Lack of coordination

Treatment

You should see your veterinarian right away because early intervention with medical or surgical care is the best way to try to prevent permanent paralysis.

Urinary Obstruction

Male pets are more prone to obstructions because their urethra (urinary tube) is longer and narrower than females. But it can occur in females as well.

Symptoms

Straining to urinate	Vomiting
Lethargy	Pain

Treatment

- Transport your pet to the nearest veterinarian or emergency clinic as soon as possible.

- Without prompt intervention, the prognosis is poor.

Chapter 9: Reproductive Emergencies

Birthing Problems/Dystocia

Dystocia is a medical term used to describe a difficult or abnormal birthing process in dogs and cats. Various factors, such as awkward position of the fetus, maternal exhaustion, a weak uterus, or a large fetus can cause it. This can be life-threatening for both the mother and the offspring if not treated promptly.

Normal Pregnancy Length

Dogs	Cats
60-63 days	63-65 days

Normal Labor for Dogs

Stage 1

The first stage typically lasts 1-12 hours and is characterized by several signs, including:

Panting	Nesting behavior	Restlessness
Shivering	Decreased appetite	Hiding

Stage 2

The second stage typically lasts between 30 minutes and 4 hours. It's characterized by the following signs:

- Abdominal contractions become more visible and frequent.

- Clear fluid may precede the birth of each puppy.

- The first puppy should arrive within 30 minutes to 4 hours once Stage 2 begins.

- Most puppies are born every 30-60 minutes, but sometimes it can take up to 2 hours.

- Puppies can be born in a breech position, which is normal for dogs.

Stage 3

- This stage involves expulsion of remaining fetal membranes, such as the placenta.

- During this time, Stage 2 and Stage 3 can alternate throughout delivery.

- Delivery of the placenta usually occurs within 5-15 min of each puppy birth.

Normal Labor for Cats

Stage 1

This is the preparatory stage and can last from a few hours up to 36 hours. During this stage, the cat may become restless, vocalize, and experience a decrease in appetite.

Stage 2

This is the active stage of labor and is characterized by the cat's water breaking and contractions beginning. Kittens are usually born within 30 minutes to 2 hours of the onset of this stage. Kittens can be born in a breech position, which is normal for cats.

Stage 3

This stage is the delivery of the placenta, which usually occurs within 5-15 minutes of each kitten's birth.

For any pet in labor, veterinary intervention is required if:

- Temperature less than 99 °F for 12-24 hours without pushing

- Part of fetal tissue showing for 15 minutes or longer without any advancement

- Green vaginal discharge without any puppies within 15 minutes

- More than 2 hours between puppy delivery

In some cases, the veterinarian may be able to use medical management, such as oxytocin injections to stimulate contractions or calcium gluconate to support muscle function. If required, surgical measures like a C-section may need to be performed to deliver the fetuses and avoid complications for both the mother and offspring.

If your pet is experiencing any difficulties during labor, such as prolonged Stage 1 or 2, or difficulty delivering a puppy or kitten, you should seek veterinary care immediately.

Eclampsia (Milk Fever)

This condition occurs more commonly in small-breed dogs with large litters, but it can affect any breed. During the development of the puppies or kittens, there is a high demand for calcium for bone formation, which can result in low blood calcium levels in the mother. It is more common in late pregnancy or during the first four weeks of nursing.

Symptoms

Panting	Restlessness	Muscle tremors
Seizures	Hyperthermia	Death possible

Treatment

- Your pet should be seen by a veterinarian as soon as possible.

- Wean puppies if old enough, or supplement them with formula.

- This can reoccur.

Prevention

- Feed the mother good quality puppy food during and after pregnancy since it's high in calcium and protein.

- Supplement puppies or kittens with a milk replacer (e.g., Esbilac) if the mother has a large litter to decrease the mother's calcium requirements.

- Supplement the mother with large litters with calcium/Tums (see p. 140 for dosing).

Mastitis

Inflammation or infection of the mammary glands, known as mastitis, can occur during nursing, during a false pregnancy, or late in pregnancy.

Symptoms

- One or more mammary glands are red, warm, swollen, firm, and are usually very painful.

- There can be pus, bloody fluid, or discolored fluid from the nipple.

- It can quickly progress to the pet developing a fever, vomiting, lethargy, and depression.

Treatment

Since most patients require antibiotics, your pet should be seen by your veterinarian. In the meantime:

- Remove puppies or kittens from the mother and feed them with a puppy or kitten milk supplement.

- Every 6-8 hours, apply warm compresses, such as a warm washcloth, to the affected gland for 5-10 minutes to help drainage.

- Cabbage leaf compresses: Apply clean, cold cabbage leaves to the affected glands for 2-3 hours. You can repeat every 6 hours.

Pyometra (Infected Uterus)

Pyometra is a dangerous condition in which the uterus fills up with pus.

- In open pyometra, the cervix is open, and there is a thick, milky discharge vaginally.

- In closed pyometra, the cervix is closed, and there is no discharge. This is typically a symptom of a much sicker animal since there is nowhere for the pus to drain.

- It can occur in older females that are not spayed.

- It occurs more commonly in dogs, but cats can also be affected.

- Typically, it happens 1-2 months after a heat cycle.

Symptoms

Drinking excessively	Urinating excessively	Lethargy
Poor appetite	Vomiting	Vaginal discharge

Treatment

The preferred treatment for pyometra is hospitalization and an emergency spay, along with IV fluids and antibiotics. However, if spaying isn't an option, particularly in the case of a prized breeding animal, alternative treatments like prostaglandins (e.g., Lutalyse®) can help relax the uterus and promote drainage. In these cases, IV fluids, antibiotics, and prostaglandins may resolve the infection without affecting the animal's breeding potential.

Be aware that side effects and complications can occur. If your dog or cat has been in heat recently and you notice any concerning symptoms, seek veterinary care immediately.

Chapter 10: Skin, Eye, Ear, Nose, and Throat Issues

Abscess

An abscess is a localized infection that results in the accumulation of pus and can be a common problem in pets, especially cats.

Causes

- Puncture/bite wound
- Foreign body
- Infection

Symptoms

Swelling	Redness
Pain	Purulent discharge (pus)

Treatment

Drainage and antibiotics are the typical means of treating an abscess.

If your pet has an abscess, there are some measures you can take to address the condition while waiting to see your veterinarian.

1. Wear gloves to avoid contact with the pus and bacteria. Restrain your pet to prevent getting bitten or scratched since an abscess can be painful.

2. Clean the abscess with a mild antiseptic solution, such as chlorhexidine or povidone-iodine, and warm water. You can use a clean cloth or gauze to clean the area gently.

3. Apply a warm compress to the abscess for 10-15 minutes several times a day. This will help soften the skin and encourage the abscess to drain.

4. Monitor your pet for signs of pain, such as limping, licking, or reluctance to move. Pain-relief medication may be prescribed by your veterinarian.

5. Encourage your pet to rest, and limit their activity to reduce further trauma to the area.

6. Do not attempt to squeeze or puncture the abscess yourself, because this can cause the infection to spread.

7. Seek veterinary care.

Your veterinarian may recommend additional treatment, such as antibiotics or surgery, depending on the severity of the abscess and underlying cause. Follow their instructions closely to ensure your pet has the best chance of a full recovery.

Anal Gland Abscess

- This can occur from trauma like a bite wound, blocked duct, excessive force when expressing the gland, or cancer.

- The anal glands are located at the 3 and 9 o'clock position around the anus.

- The area is generally very swollen and painful. Dogs may scoot.

Treatment

1. Apply a warm compress to the area.

2. Clean with a disinfectant like chlorhexidine or povidone-iodine, and then apply a triple antibiotic ointment like Neosporin every 12 hours.

3. Apply an Elizabethan collar (see p. 29) to prevent licking.

4. Make an appointment with your veterinarian.

5. Pain medicine, antibiotics, or even surgery may be needed.

Anaphylactic Shock

Also known as anaphylaxis, this can be a life-threatening condition. It's a severe allergic reaction to bug bites or vaccinations (uncommon).

Symptoms in Dogs

Diarrhea (may have blood)	Swelling	Collapse

Symptoms for Cats

Vomiting	Diarrhea	Drooling
Swelling	Trouble breathing	Itching around face

Treatment

- If possible, give one dose of Benadryl based on your pet's weight (see p. 137).

- Transport immediately to the closest veterinarian.

Eye Issues

Eye problems can be serious and cause blindness if not addressed right away. Here are the most common eye conditions:

Allergies

Both food allergies and seasonal allergies can lead to eye redness and discharge.

Cataracts

This occurs when the lens of the eye turns white and can lead to blindness.

Chemical in the Eye

Chemicals can burn the eye and cause ulcers, and there is risk of the eye rupturing. It can lead to redness, pain, and even blindness if not treated as soon as possible.

Treatment

- If an irritant, such as a chemical or other product, unintentionally comes into contact with the eye, rinse the eye thoroughly with a continuous stream of saline solution or contact lens saline solution.

- For a homemade saline solution, mix 2 teaspoons of table salt into 1 quart of water, and use for at least 15 minutes.

- Seek veterinary care right away.

Cherry Eye (Third Eyelid Prolapse)

- Certain breeds are more prone (bulldog, pug).

- Cherry eye occurs when cartilage around the eye is weak and the third eyelid rolls up.

- Surgery is usually the only way to treat it (sometimes the eyelids will go back on their own, but this is rare).

Corneal Ulcer (Scratch on the Eye)

Scratches on the eye are usually caused by a foreign body like foxtail or dirt.

- The eye can be cloudy and can even rupture if not treated appropriately.

- Symptoms include discharge, squinting, and pain.

Treatment

Apply sterile eye lubricant (artificial tears) to the affected eye every 4 hours to help with irritation, and schedule an appointment right away with your veterinarian.

If you can see a foreign object like a foxtail, you can have someone hold your pet's head very still. Using tweezers, gently try to remove the object. If this is not possible, your pet should be seen right away to avoid more pain, irritation, and possible ulceration of the eye.

Dry Eye (KCS: Keratoconjunctivitis Sicca)

Dry eye happens when the eyes don't produce enough tears. This can lead to a thick discharge, redness, and irritation or pain.

Eyelid Issues

- **Ectropion:** The lower eyelids are droopy, causing dry, irritated eyes along with excess tearing and discharge.

- **Entropion:** Eyelids roll inwards toward the eye and cause irritation to the eye along with discharge, excess tearing, and redness.

Glaucoma

Glaucoma is caused by high pressure in the eye that can lead to blindness. The eyes can become enlarged, and the condition can be painful.

Infection

Symptoms like discharge, redness, and pain could indicate an infection.

Perforation

A perforation, or piercing, of the eye is usually caused by trauma. This painful condition can lead to blindness, and the eyes may need to be removed if not treated by a veterinarian as soon as possible.

Proptosis (Eye out of Socket)

- This painful condition usually occurs from trauma. The eyelid won't close over the eye. Here's how you can help your pet until you can reach a veterinarian:

- Lubricate the eye with a sterile eye lubricant, such as contact lens wetting solution, K-Y jelly, or water.

- Transport to nearest veterinary clinic.

Treatment

If you cannot be seen by a veterinarian within 1-2 hours, you can try to replace the eye:

- Use K-Y jelly generously over the eye and eyelids.

- Gently grab onto the lower and upper eyelids and pull the eyelids straight up.

- You can use a Q-tip to grab the edges of the upper and lower eyelids.

- The eyeball should go back in.

- Do not forcefully push it back in.

- If it doesn't go in proceed to the nearest veterinary clinic.

- The longer the eye is out of the socket, the higher the risk of permanent blindness, and the eye may need to be removed.

Other Eye Issues

An autoimmune disease, trauma to the eyelid, or issues with the retina may also affect your pet's eyes.

Fishhooks & Fishing Line

If your pet gets impaled by a fishing hook:

- You cannot just pull the hook through since the barb will get stuck in the skin.

- First, muzzle your pet if you can (see p. 2) or have someone restrain them.

- Cut off the barbed end of the looped end with metal cutters.

- Using a hemostat or pliers, gently pull the hook through.

- Clean the area with a disinfectant like chlorhexidine or povidone-iodine, and apply a triple antibiotic ointment like Neosporin to the wound twice a day for 2-3 days.

- If you are unable to remove the fishhook safely, then take your pet to a veterinarian for removal.

If your pet ingests a fishing line:

- Do not try to pull out the fishing line coming out of the mouth or out of the anus.

- These can get entangled in the intestines and can cause an obstruction or tearing.

- Take your pet in right away to be seen by a veterinarian.

Head Shaking

Causes

- Ear infection

- Allergies

- Foreign body (such as foxtail)

Because there are many possible causes, schedule an appointment with your veterinarian. Here's what you can do in the meantime:

Inner Ear Infections

- **Check eyes for flickering:** If your pet's eyes are flickering left or right, it could indicate an inner ear infection, which requires medical treatment.

- **Give nausea medication:** Pets with inner ear infections may tilt their head, lose balance, vomit, or refuse to eat due to nausea (similar to vertigo). You can give meclizine (e.g., Dramamine) for nausea (see page 143 for dosage) and schedule an appointment with your veterinarian.

- **Start a bland diet** (see p. 97).

External Ear Infections

- **Signs:** You may notice discharge or a foul smell coming from their ears.
- **Action:** Schedule an appointment with your veterinarian, because these infections typically require topical ear medications to treat yeast and/or bacteria.

Warning: Prolonged or intense head shaking can lead to an ear hematoma (a fluid-filled pocket between the skin and cartilage). This usually requires surgical treatment but can sometimes be managed medically.

Hives

Hives are raised, red, itchy spots that can occur all over the body or just be confined to one area. It's an allergic reaction that typically occurs after a bug bite or after something your pet has eaten or been in contact with.

Treatment

- Give a dose of Benadryl based on your pet's weight (see p. 143).

- Soak your pet cool water to help calm the itch.

- Oatmeal or aloe shampoo or conditioner sometimes helps.

- You may need to repeat the Benadryl every 12 hours for 2-3 days.

- If there's no improvement or the hives get worse, or if your pet has trouble breathing, transfer to a veterinarian.

Hot Spot

A hot spot, also known as acute moist dermatitis, is a painful and itchy skin condition that can affect dogs and cats.

Here are some steps you can take to treat a hot spot in your pet:

1. Trim the fur around the hot spot to expose the affected area to allow airflow so it can dry out.

2. Clean the area with a gentle, pet-safe cleanser or antiseptic solution to remove dirt, debris, or bacteria.

3. Apply a topical treatment such as a medicated cream, spray, or ointment to soothe the skin, reduce inflammation, and promote healing. Your veterinarian may recommend a specific product based on the severity of the hot spot. Some products over the counter, such as a triple antibiotic ointment, can suffice.

4. Use an Elizabethan collar (see p. 29) or a cone to prevent your pet from licking or biting the affected area, which can worsen the condition.

5. Monitor your pet closely for signs of improvement or worsening of the hot spot, and seek veterinary care if necessary.

In addition to these steps, it's important to identify and address the underlying cause of the hot spot, which may include flea or tick infestations, allergies, or skin irritations. Your veterinarian can help you determine the underlying cause and provide appropriate treatment, such as flea preventives, dietary changes, or allergy medications.

Nosebleed

Causes

Foreign body	Infection	Cancer
Trauma	High blood pressure	Toxin

Treatment

1. Keep your pet calm.

2. Apply an ice pack or bag of frozen peas/vegetables to the nose for 5-10 minutes at a time.

3. If the nose continues to bleed, you should be seen by a veterinarian.

Porcupine Quills

- These should be removed by your veterinarian.

- If the entire quill isn't removed, it can cause infection or migrate further into the body.

- They are painful to remove, so your pet typically needs to be sedated or anesthetized.

Prolapse

A prolapse refers to internal tissue that falls out of the body (everted) to the outside.

- **Vaginal prolapse:** This can occur when a dog is in heat or pregnant.

- **Rectal prolapse:** This can occur from straining (constipation or diarrhea), parasites, tumors, or a foreign body.

Treatment

Surgery is usually needed for prolapsed tissue. In the meantime, you can try doing the following:

1. Clean the everted tissue gently with cool water.

2. Mix cool water with a large amount of granulated sugar. Soak the prolapsed tissue in the sugar solution for 15 minutes.

3. Using gloves and a lot of lubricant, gently push the vaginal or rectal tissue back in. If you can't get it back in or it comes back out, you should take your pet to a veterinarian.

4. If the tissue is black or brown, you should not try to replace it.

5. Schedule an appointment to be seen by your veterinarian as soon as possible.

Reverse Sneezing

- Reverse sneezing is a spasm that causes sneezing and snorting at the same time.

- Your pet may put their head down and spread their front legs while it is occurring.

- It's usually benign and can occur from allergies.

- If it continues, a foreign body (like foxtail), parasites, or (less likely) a mass should be ruled out by a veterinarian.

Treatment

1. Lay your pet on their back and rub their throat.

2. Close both nostrils so they will swallow, which usually stops the spasm if it's a reverse sneeze.

3. If it continues, you should seek veterinary care to ensure there is nothing else going on.

Skunk Spray

Here's a home recipe* for skunk odor removal. Mix together:

- 1 quart 3% hydrogen peroxide

- 1/4 cup baking soda

- 1 teaspoon of liquid dish soap or hand soap

Or you can buy a commercial OTC product, such as Thornell's Skunk Off.

Bathing Directions**

1. Lather your pet in warm water, and coat your pet with the solution you made or bought, concentrating on the skunked areas.

2. Work it into the fur and leave it on for 5 minutes, making sure not to get it into their eyes.

3. You may need to repeat until the smell is gone.

4. Rinse with warm water.

5. Discard any remaining solution down the sink.

Do not smoke around your dog or the mixed solution because the mixture is flammable.

**The bathing solution may change the coat color in black-coated dogs.*

Skunk Toxic Shock Syndrome

- This is a rare condition that can occur within 12-24 hours of being sprayed.

- It can cause life-threatening anemia.

Symptoms

Lethargy	Vomiting	Black stool
Pale gums	Loss of appetite	

If you notice any of these symptoms, please go to your veterinarian immediately.

Sneezing

Though sneezing is common in pets, if your pet sneezes and you see blood, or if it's violent enough that they hit their head on the ground, they may have something like a foxtail or foreign body in their nose.

Foxtail

Take your pet to your veterinarian or ER clinic. They almost always need to be sedated to scope their nose and remove the foreign body.

Chapter 11: Digestive Upset

Constipation

Causes

Eating indigestible items like bones	Dehydration	Pain from things like arthritis
Obesity	Certain medications	Obstructions

Symptoms

Not eating	Vomiting	Pain
Diarrhea	Straining to defecate	

Treatment

If symptoms are mild, try these options:

- Metamucil (1-4 tsp mixed with food every 12-24 hours)

- Fiber cereal, such as Fiber One or All-Bran (1-2 tbsp mixed with food every 12-24 hours)

- Canned pumpkin

- Bland diet (see p. 97)

Enemas

- Do not try to perform an enema at home. Risk of colon rupture can occur.

- Some OTC enema brands like Fleet can contain sodium phosphate, which can be toxic to dogs and cats.

If your pet is vomiting or not eating, they should be seen by your veterinarian.

Diarrhea

Diarrhea can be caused by parasites, toxins, stress, or dietary indiscretion, such as getting into the trash or eating human food. There are two kinds of diarrhea:

Small Bowel Diarrhea

Symptoms

Increase in frequency and/or volume of defecation	Smaller quantity than normal	Soft or partially formed feces
Mucus	Dark red blood present	No straining

Treatment

- Pepto-Bismol (see p. 139)

- Fecal analysis at your veterinarian's

- A probiotic, such as Purina Pro Plan FortiFlora, Proviable, and Culturelle (see p. 141)

Large Bowel Diarrhea

Symptoms

Increase in frequency and/or urgency of defecation	Smaller quantity than normal	Watery
Mucus	Red blood present	Straining

Treatment

- Metamucil (1-4 tsp mixed with food every 12 -24 hours) or a fiber cereal, such as Fiber One or All-Bran (⅛ cup to each meal; see p. 142)

- Alternatively, a bland, high fiber diet (see p. 97)

- A probiotic, such as Purina Pro Plan FortiFlora, Proviable, and Culturelle (see p. 141)

- Imodium (see p. 141)

If your pet is not eating or is acting lethargic, or if the diarrhea isn't improving within 24-36 hours, they should be seen by a veterinarian. Take a fresh stool sample with you to the appointment so a fecal test can be performed.

Gastritis

Gastritis is the inflammation and irritation of the stomach lining.

Causes

Bacterial or viral infection	Dietary indiscretion	Food allergies
Foreign bodies	Some medications	

Symptoms

Vomiting	Diarrhea	Dehydration	Lethargy
Loss of appetite	Pale gums	Abdominal pain	Bloody stool

Treatment For Mild Symptoms

- Withhold food and water for 12-24 hours to allow the stomach to rest and heal.

- Administer antiemetic (anti-nausea) and antacid medications to alleviate vomiting and gastric irritation.

- Feed a bland diet (see p. 97).

Treatment for Severe Symptoms

If your pet continues to vomit, doesn't eat, or is lethargic, they should be seen by your veterinarian. Treatments for more severe symptoms may include these:

- Provide fluid therapy and electrolyte replacement to correct dehydration and electrolyte imbalances.

- Treat the underlying cause of gastritis, such as bacterial infection or food allergy.

Consult a veterinarian if you suspect your dog has gastritis or is experiencing any gastrointestinal symptoms. In severe cases, gastritis can lead to dehydration, electrolyte imbalances, and other complications.

Pancreatitis

This is a medical condition in which the pancreas becomes inflamed, leading to digestive problems and other complications. It can affect both dogs and cats.

Symptoms

Vomiting	Lethargy	Diarrhea	Dehydration
Loss of appetite	Fever	Abdominal pain	Jaundice (yellowing skin or eyes)

Causes

The exact cause of pancreatitis is not always known, but some factors that may contribute to its development include:

High-fat diet	Obesity	Trauma or injury to the pancreas
Certain medications or toxins	Infection	Genetics

Treatment

Treatment for pancreatitis in pets typically involves supportive care from a veterinarian to manage symptoms and help the pancreas heal. This may include:

- Fasting to give the pancreas rest

- Intravenous (IV) fluids to prevent dehydration and maintain electrolyte balance

- Pain medication to manage discomfort

- Anti-nausea medication to control vomiting

- Nutritional support with a low-fat bland diet (see p. 97)

- Antibiotics if there is an infection present

Consult with a veterinarian right away if you suspect your pet has pancreatitis, because early intervention can help avoid complications like diabetes and improve the chances of recovery.

Parvo

Canine parvovirus is a highly contagious viral disease that affects dogs, especially puppies. It attacks the gastrointestinal tract and causes severe vomiting, diarrhea, and dehydration. It can also damage the immune system, leaving the dog vulnerable to other infections.

The virus is spread through contact with infected dogs or contaminated surfaces, such as bedding, food and water bowls, and feces. Puppies are at the highest risk of contracting the virus, but any dog can become infected. Puppies are not fully vaccinated against parvovirus until they have had 3-4 parvo vaccines starting at 6-8 weeks until 16 weeks (3-4 weeks apart).

Symptoms

Lethargy	Diarrhea, which can be bloody
Vomiting	Not eating

Treatment

Treatment for parvo typically involves hospitalization and supportive care, because there is no specific cure for the virus. The main goals of treatment are to control vomiting and diarrhea, replace fluids and electrolytes, and prevent secondary infections.

Here are some things you can do at home to support your dog's recovery:

- **Keep your dog hydrated:** One of the most critical aspects of treating parvo is keeping your dog hydrated. Give your dog small, frequent amounts of fresh, clean water or unflavored Pedialyte to help replenish lost fluids and minerals.

- **Provide small, frequent meals:** Give your dog a bland diet (see p. 97).

- **Adjust diet if your dog is vomiting:** If they are vomiting, withhold food for 4 hours, then try again with a small amount of bland food.

- **Keep a close eye on your dog's symptoms:** Watch out for vomiting and diarrhea, and report any changes to your veterinarian. They may need to adjust your dog's treatment plan or provide additional supportive care.

- **Isolate your dog:** Parvo is highly contagious and can easily spread to other dogs. Keep your infected dog isolated from other pets, and disinfect any areas or objects with a diluted bleach solution that may have come into contact with their bodily fluids.

You'll need to work closely with your veterinarian to ensure your dog receives proper treatment for parvo. Home remedies should be used only in conjunction with veterinary care and under the guidance of your veterinarian.

Prevention

Prevention is the best approach to parvo. Puppies should be vaccinated against the virus, and all dogs should be kept away from infected dogs and contaminated areas. If you suspect your dog may have parvo, seek veterinary care immediately. Early treatment can greatly improve the chances of survival.

Vomiting

- Vomiting can be caused by dietary indiscretion (eating human food, garbage, etc.), ingesting a foreign object, parasites, or toxin.

- Withhold food and water for 12 hours.

- If they only vomited once and are otherwise acting normal, you can try a bland diet (see p. 97). If they continue to vomit or are acting lethargic, schedule an appointment right away with your veterinarian.

Bland Diet Instructions

These diet options* will work for both dogs and cats:

- Combine low-fat cottage cheese and boiled white rice in a 1:3 ratio.
- Use boiled chicken or hamburger along with cooked white rice or pasta.
- Choose baby food without onion or garlic mixed with boiled white rice.
- Serve chicken or beef broth without onion or garlic, poured over boiled white rice.

Feeding Guidelines

1. Withhold food and water for 4-6 hours. If vomiting occurs within this period, wait 4-6 hours before trying again.

2. If there is no vomiting during the initial period, start offering small amounts of the bland diet every 4 hours, using the following scale:

   - Cats and small dogs weighing less than 20 pounds: 1-3 tablespoons
   - Dogs weighing 20-40 pounds: ¼ to ½ cup
   - Dogs weighing over 40 pounds: ½ to ¾ cup

3. Provide small amounts of water, Pedialyte, or ice cubes. Avoid large quantities because it may cause more vomiting.

4. Once the vomiting or diarrhea has completely resolved (usually in 1-2 days), gradually reintroduce your pet's regular diet. Mix the regular food with the bland diet, increasing the proportion of the regular diet by 25% each day until your pet is fully transitioned back to regular food.

These diets are for temporary use only and do not meet nutritional requirements for long-term use.

Chapter 12: Common Household Toxins for Pets

Ant Traps

If the ant trap has arsenic in it, call Animal Poison Control and/or go to your veterinarian immediately.

- If the active ingredient is borax, there's a wide safety margin for pets.

- If the active ingredient is avermectin, there's also a wide safety margin, with the exception of collie breeds—they are more sensitive, and you should call Animal Poison Control.

- A bigger concern is typically the plastic case of the ant trap causing an issue with irritation or obstruction.

- The ingredients can cause GI irritation.

Treatment

Start a high-fiber, bland diet (see p. 97), and monitor for vomiting, diarrhea, and lethargy. Consult with your veterinarian if any of these symptoms occur.

Antifreeze

Antifreeze toxicity is a serious condition that can be fatal without early treatment. The toxicity is caused by ethylene glycol, which can lead to kidney failure and neurological damage. Unfortunately, pets are particularly at risk of ingesting antifreeze because it has a sweet taste.

Antifreeze can be found in a variety of household items, including the base of portable basketball hoops, toilets to winterize a house and prevent plumbing from freezing, printer and pen inks, eye masks, snow globes, and some household latex paints.

Symptoms

Loss of balance	Loss of appetite	Vomiting	Depression
Increased thirst and urination	Seizures	Coma	Death possible

Treatment

Immediate veterinary care is crucial if you suspect your pet has ingested antifreeze because treatment is time-sensitive and can greatly improve the chances of a positive outcome.

Arsenic

Arsenic can be found in ash from burnt wood, treated wood, some rat baits, certain herbicides and insecticides, and some insulation.

Symptoms

Vomiting	Diarrhea	Painful abdomen	Staggering
Weakness	Drooling	Dehydration	Death possible

Treatment

- Transport immediately to the nearest veterinary clinic.

- Usual treatments include inducing vomiting and giving activated charcoal.

- Fluid therapy and chelation therapy, which binds the poison, may also be used.

- The prognosis may not be good without immediate and aggressive therapy.

Battery Ingestion

When a battery is punctured, corrosive substances may leak out, leading to the risk of severe burns and ulcers in the mouth and digestive tract. In some cases, these burns can be so severe that they may rupture the esophagus or intestines. Additionally, there is a possibility of heavy metal poisoning if a battery remains in the digestive tract for more than 2-3 days.

Treatment

- If you observe your pet chewing on a battery, take immediate action by removing the battery and rinsing their mouth thoroughly for 15-20 minutes.

- Ensure that your pet's head is facing downward to prevent water from entering the throat or trachea.

- Afterward, seek veterinary care promptly.

- If you suspect that your pet has swallowed a battery, seek immediate veterinary attention.

- A radiograph can be taken at the veterinary hospital to determine if the battery has been ingested. Surgery may be required to safely remove the battery, because inducing vomiting is not recommended in such cases.

- Other treatments typically include antacids, pain medication, and a bland diet to help your pet's recovery.

Bleach

Bleach commonly contains 3-6% hypochlorite. Dogs may sometimes ingest bleach or come into contact with it on their skin.

- Bleach that has higher than 6% concentration of hypochlorite can cause burns to the gums and throat.

- Color-safe bleaches usually contain hydrogen peroxide, which can cause persistent vomiting.

Symptoms

These are the possible symptoms if your pet ingests bleach:

Vomiting	Diarrhea
Drooling	Respiratory irritation

These are the possible symptoms if your pet inhales bleach fumes:

Coughing	Wheezing
Trouble breathing	

Treatment

- Move your pet to fresh air.
- Rinse the mouth and face with cool water.
- Offer your pet milk to help dilute the bleach and coat the throat and stomach.
- If bleach is on their skin or coat, bathe them with liquid dishwashing detergent until the bleach smell is gone.
- Monitor for digestive upset.

If your pet continues to vomit, or has respiratory distress, or if the bleach concentration is greater than 6%, you should take them to the emergency clinic right away.

Desiccant Packets and Oxygen Absorbers

These are frequently found in food products, medications, clothing, and electronics. They're used to absorb moisture and/or oxygen to prevent spoilage or damage to products.

Desiccant Packets

- Made of silicon dioxide beads

- Can be different colors

- Used to absorb moisture

- Inert and non-toxic

- Mild digestive upset possible

Oxygen Absorbers

- Can include iron at low doses

- Typically a brown to black powder

- Usually inert

- Mild digestive upset possible

If the packaging on either is ingested, it may irritate the GI tract or cause a blockage.

Treatment

- Start a high fiber diet for a few days to help push the packaging through the GI tract and to help with any digestive upset.

- If a large amount of desiccant packets or oxygen absorbers are ingested, you should consult your veterinarian or Animal Poison Control because higher doses can cause electrolyte imbalances and iron toxicity in some cases.

Always keep desiccant packets and oxygen absorbers out of reach of pets to prevent accidental ingestion.

Essential Oils

Essential oils are common in many households. Certain oils can be toxic to both dogs and cats if ingested, applied topically, or inhaled.

Some common essential oils that are toxic include pine, citrus, clove, eucalyptus, hyssop, peppermint, tea tree, wintergreen, and citronella oil.

Symptoms

Vomiting	Diarrhea	Oral ulcers	Drooling
Hyperthermia	Liver toxicity	Skin irritation	Hypertension
Depression	Seizures	Coma	

Treatment

Since there is no antidote for essential oil exposure, it is recommended to transport to a veterinarian right away. Treatment consists of supportive care to manage symptoms.

Fur Contaminants - Oil

Using Dawn dishwashing liquid, you can remove most oily substances, including motor oil, from the coat. Lather the coat well for 10 minutes, and rinse to remove.

Gorilla Glue® (Polyurethane Glue)

Polyurethane adhesives that contain diphenylmethane diisocyanate (MDI) can be dangerous if ingested by pets. Examples include Gorilla Glue, Elmer's ProBond, and Selleys Aquadhere Durabond.

When ingested, it can expand and harden in the stomach, causing a blockage or obstruction.

Treatment

- Transfer to a veterinarian immediately.

- Surgical intervention may be necessary to remove the hardened glue from the digestive tract.

Always keep all adhesives and household chemicals out of reach of pets to prevent accidental ingestion.

Ocean Water Ingestion/Salt Toxicity

This occurs after drinking too much seawater or consuming too much salt.

Symptoms

Vomiting	Diarrhea	Excessive thirst
Lethargy	Loss of appetite	Dehydration
Trembling	Confusion	Seizures

Treatment

- Offer your pet fresh water.

- Watch your dog closely for any signs of dehydration or other symptoms.

- Start a bland diet (see p. 97).

- Provide electrolytes, either with a specially formulated electrolyte solution designed for dogs or with a mixture of water and low-sodium chicken broth or Pedialyte.

- If your dog shows more severe symptoms, such as seizures or loss of consciousness, seek veterinary attention immediately.

- Hospitalization may be necessary to provide intravenous fluids and medications to help with dehydration and other symptoms.

Prevention

Always monitor your pets closely when they are near the water. Providing plenty of fresh water for them to drink and letting them have minimal exposure to the salt water will help prevent accidental ingestion.

Overdose of Prescribed Pet Medication

If the overdose occurred within an hour of giving the medication, and your dog is not showing any symptoms, you can try to induce vomiting with hydrogen peroxide (see p. 148).

If symptoms are already occurring, you should immediately transport your pet to the nearest emergency clinic.

Overdose of Topical Flea Medication

Pyrethrin/Pyrethroid (Flea Control for Cats) and Permethrin (Flea Control for Dogs)

It is not uncommon for owners to put the wrong weight flea control on their pet, which can cause an overdose. And sometimes an owner will accidentally use a dog's flea treatment, which contains permethrin, on a cat. Permethrin is toxic to cats.

Symptoms

Salivating	Hyper- or hypothermia	Vomiting
Tremors	Difficulty breathing	Seizures
Weakness	Death possible	

Treatment

Immediately bathe your pet in Dawn dishwashing liquid. The detergent helps pull up the oil-based flea control and remove it. If the symptoms are mild or haven't begun yet, then this usually stops or prevents symptoms. But if your pet shows more advanced symptoms like weakness, difficulty breathing, or seizures, you should immediately transport them to your nearest emergency veterinary clinic.

Rodenticides (Rat and Mouse Bait)

Rodenticides are baits used to control rats and mice, and they come in an anticoagulant form that stops blood from clotting. There are different active ingredients, with brodifacoum, bromadiolone, difethialone, and difenacoum being the most toxic.

Diphacinone, chlorophacinone, warfarin, coumatetralyl, coumafuryl (Fumarin), pindone, and valone are less toxic. They also come in a neurotoxic form (bromethalin). which is much more toxic.

Rodenticides: Anticoagulant Form

This type of rat bait stops blood from clotting.

Symptoms

Symptoms may take 3-7 days to appear.

Bleeding anywhere	Coughing	Difficulty breathing
Bruising	Lethargy	Weakness

Treatment

- If ingestion occurred within 4 hours AND your pet's not showing symptoms, you can induce vomiting with hydrogen peroxide (see p. 148). Then, take them to the local clinic.

- If nothing comes up, proceed to the emergency clinic.

- There is an antidote (vitamin K), and the prognosis is good if they are treated early.

Rodenticides: Neurotoxic Form

This is much more toxic than the anticoagulant form of rodenticides.

Symptoms

It can take hours to days for symptoms to appear.

Hyperexcitable	Hyperthermia	Muscle tremors
Seizures	Death possible	

Treatment

- Proceed to the nearest emergency clinic immediately.

- Prognosis is poor without immediate treatment, and there is NO antidote.

Snail Bait (Metaldehyde)

Snail bait is used to control slugs and snails, and it comes in the form of pellets, liquids, powders, granules, and gels. Metaldehyde is the most common ingredient. Some formulations contain molasses, which attracts dogs and cats.

Symptoms

Symptoms can occur within 30 minutes to 3 hours after ingestion.

Vomiting	Diarrhea	Drooling
Anxiety /restlessness	Ataxia/loss of balance	Tremors
Seizures	Hyperthermia	Depression
Liver failure	Blindness	Death possible

Treatment

Immediate transport to the nearest veterinarian for treatment is necessary. Inducing vomiting at home is not recommended because symptoms progress rapidly. Decontamination should only be performed by your veterinarian.

Zinc Phosphide (Gopher Bait)

Zinc phosphide is used to kill gophers, moles, and other rodents. It's usually in pellet form and smells like garlic or rotten fish. When it's ingested, the stomach acid converts it to phosphine gas, which is toxic to both pets and people.

Symptoms

Symptoms occur within 15 minutes to 4 hours.

Anxiety/ agitation	Lethargy	Vocalization
Tremors/ seizures	Trouble breathing/coughing	Loss of balance
Blue gums	Vomiting and possibly blood	Death possible

Treatment

- **Do not induce vomiting.** Phosphine gas will be released into the environment, which is toxic to pets and people.

- Transport to the nearest veterinary clinic with windows down for ventilation.

The prognosis depends on how much your pet ingested and how long ago it was. Early treatment gives your pet the best chance of survival.

Chapter 13: Common Drug Ingestions

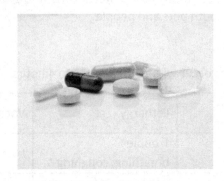

It is important to keep any medicines out of your pet's reach.

Amphetamines

These include legal pharmaceuticals to treat obesity, ADHD, and narcolepsy in people (Adipex-P, Adderall, Ritalin, Vyvanse, dextroamphetamine, lisdexamfetamine, dexmethylphenidate, dextroamphetamine, methylphenidate) and illegal or abused substances (methamphetamine, ecstasy, bath salts).

Symptoms

Symptoms occur within 30-60 minutes.

Hyperactivity	Aggression	Eyes dilated
Disoriented	Restlessness	Loss of balance
Tremors	High heart rate	High respiratory rate
Agitation	Seizures	Low heart rate, weakness, and depression (uncommon)

Treatment

- Induce vomiting (see p. 148) if the medication was ingested within 20 minutes and your dog is not showing symptoms.

- If you are unable to induce vomiting or your pet is showing signs of toxicity, transport them to the nearest veterinary clinic.

Antidepressants

The most prescribed are SSRIs like sertraline (Zoloft) and fluoxetine (Prozac).

Symptoms

Lethargy/ depression	Tremors	Disoriented
Loss of balance	Fever (hyperthermia)	Neurological signs

Treatment

- If ingestion occurs within 1 hour, try inducing vomiting (see p. 148) if not showing symptoms.

- If it has been longer than 1 hour or you're unable to induce vomiting, transport to your local veterinary clinic ASAP.

Asthma Inhalers

Asthma inhalers typically have medications like albuterol or salbutamol in them. Dogs can accidentally chew and puncture the inhaler, leading to a life-threatening toxic ingestion.

Symptoms

Racing heart	Bright red gums	Vomiting
Dilated pupils	Agitation	Weakness
Severe arrythmia	Collapse	Death possible

Treatment

- Immediately transfer your pet to a veterinary emergency clinic.
- Treatment usually consists of IV fluids, electrolyte supplementation, anti-arrythmia medications, and sedatives.
- Treatment typically requires 24-36 hours of care until symptoms subside.

Cocaine

Cocaine is absorbed rapidly through the mouth and digestive tract. It's highly toxic even in small doses.

Symptoms

Hyperactivity	Aggression	Loss of balance	Vomiting
Drooling	Hyperthermia/ fever	Tremors	Seizures
High heart rate	High respiratory rate	Death possible	

Treatment

Immediately transfer your pet to an emergency clinic.

Ibuprofen

Ibuprofen, found in OTC pain relievers like Advil, Motrin, and Midol, can affect the kidneys and intestines.

Symptoms

Vomiting	Diarrhea (can be black)	Not eating
Drinking excessively	Lethargy	Loss of balance
Bleeding	Seizures	Coma

Treatment

- If ingestion occurs within 20 minutes and your dog is not showing symptoms, you can induce vomiting (see p. 148).

- If they're showing symptoms or it has been longer than 20 minutes, then transport to your local veterinary hospital.

Marijuana/Cannabis

Marijuana contains **THC**, which is harmful to pets.

Symptoms

Symptoms begin in 30-90 minutes and can last for days.

Lack of coordination	Listlessness	Pupils dilated
Slow heart rate	Dribble urine sometimes	

Treatment

- If ingested in less than 30 minutes, give your pet peroxide to induce vomiting (see p. 148). This is not recommended after 30 minutes.

- Charcoal can be administered (see p. 145).

- Put your pet in a confined area where you can monitor them and where they cannot hurt themselves (fall downstairs, etc.).

- If your pet is sedated and difficult to arouse, they should be evaluated by a veterinarian as soon as possible.

Nicotine

E-Cigarettes

E-cigarettes contain liquid nicotine, which can be toxic to pets even in small amounts.

- Symptoms occur within 15-20 minutes since nicotine is absorbed rapidly.

- Battery ingestion is also possible if your pet swallows the entire e-cigarette, which can lead to burns in the mouth or esophagus and/or a foreign body obstruction (see p. 57).

- E-cigarettes may contain xylitol, which is highly toxic (see p. 54).

Cigarettes and Chewing Tobacco

Symptoms appear within 30-90 minutes.

Symptoms

Vomiting	Diarrhea	Drooling	Tremors
Agitation	Weakness	Low heart rate	High heart rate
Low respiratory rate	Seizures	Coma	Death possible

Treatment

- Seek veterinary attention immediately.

- Your veterinarian may induce vomiting to remove any remaining nicotine from the stomach, administer activated charcoal to help prevent absorption, and provide supportive care to manage any symptoms.

Opioids and Opiates

Examples include hydrocodone, oxycodone, morphine, codeine, and fentanyl, though there are many more.

Symptoms

Depression	Loss of balance	Vomiting	Seizures
Breathing too slowly or shallowly	Low heart rate	Cats: overexcited	Cats: difficulty urinating

Treatment

- If ingested within 2 hours and no symptoms are present, induce vomiting (see p. 148). NEVER induce vomiting if showing symptoms.

- Administer naloxone if available intranasally (into the nose), and transport to a veterinary clinic as soon as possible. If they stop breathing, start CPR (see p. 14).

- Naloxone is free through most health departments, or you can purchase through many pharmacies. It would make a great addition to your pet first aid kit.

Tylenol (Acetaminophen, Paracetamol)

Tylenol can be toxic to your pet's liver, kidneys, and blood. Cats have an even higher risk of toxicity.

Symptoms

Anorexia	Lethargy	Vomiting	Loss of balance
Skin yellowing	Fainting	Drinking excessively	Stupor
Blue or brown gums	Trouble breathing	Swelling of face or feet	Weakness
Painful abdomen	Bruising	Hypothermia	

Treatment

- If less than 20 minutes since the ingestion, you can induce vomiting (see p. 148).

- If longer than 20 minutes or if your pet is showing symptoms, transfer to a veterinary clinic immediately. Treatment usually consists of decontamination, medications to bind the drug, fluid therapy, and supportive care. Prognosis is uncertain unless treatment is aggressive and done quickly.

For Other Medications

Contact the Pet Poison Helpline® at (855) 764-7661.

Chapter 14: Insects, Arachnids, Snakes, and Toads

Bee/Wasp Sting

If your pet has been stung by a bee or wasp, it can be painful and scary for them.

Symptoms

Bee stings in dogs typically cause noticeable swelling around the sting site within a few minutes.

Pain	Vomiting/ diarrhea	Itchiness
Swelling around bite	Difficulty breathing	Collapse

Treatment

- **Remove the stinger:** If you can see the stinger, use a pair of tweezers to remove it. Be careful not to squeeze the stinger, because this can release more venom.

- **Give Benadryl:** See chart for dose on page 192. You may need to repeat the Benadryl every 12 hours for 2-3 days.

- **Use a cold compress:** Apply a cold compress to the area for 10-15 minutes to help reduce swelling and pain. You can use a bag of frozen vegetables or a towel soaked in cold water.

- **Watch for signs of an allergic reaction:** Some pets can have a severe allergic reaction and difficulty breathing.

- If vomiting or difficulty breathing occurs, you should take your pet to see your veterinarian immediately.

- If your pet is acting normal, and the swelling is going down but not completely gone in 12 hours, you can give another dose of Benadryl.

Prevention

Try to keep your pet away from bees or other stinging insects, and use insect-repellent products made for pets.

Fleas

- Fleas are common insects that can be found on dogs and cats.

- They have 4 life stages: egg, larva, pupa, and adult.

- They can lay up to 50 eggs per day and live for months.

- Fleas can carry *Bartonella* bacteria, which causes cat scratch disease, along with plague, tapeworms, and flea-borne typhus.

- Fleas are more common in spring and fall, though depending on where you live, they could be present year-round.

- Tapeworms can be transmitted to animals or people by swallowing an infected flea. This is more common in children.

- Fleas can cause flea allergy dermatitis, which typically presents as scabs along the lower back and sores.

- Fleas leave behind their "dirt" (stool), a black substance that, if you add water to, will turn red.

Prevention

Here's how you can get rid of fleas and keep them away:

- **Flea control for pets:** Use a flea medication like Bravecto, Revolution, Advantage, Seresto, NexGard, or Trifexis. Be sure to treat all the pets in your household.

- **Environmental treatments:** Treat the environment for fleas with a flea powder like Fleabusters, especially in carpeted areas of your house. Vacuum frequently, especially under sofas and tables. Be sure to clean out the vacuum and throw the bag away.

Ticks

Learn to recognize these species of ticks that carry disease:

American Dog Tick/Wood Tick
(*Dermacentor variabilis*)

The male is on the left, and the female on the right.

Deer Tick/Black-legged Tick
(*Ixodes scapularis*)

Brown Dog Tick
(*Rhipicephalus sanguineus*)

Gulf Coast Tick
(*Amblyomma maculatum*)

Lone Star Tick
(*Amblyomma americanum*)

Rocky Mountain Wood Tick
(*Dermacentor andersoni*)

Western Black-Legged Tick
(*Ixodes pacificus*)

How to Remove a Tick

1. You will need gloves, tweezers, and rubbing alcohol or other disinfectant.

2. With gloves on, use tweezers to grasp the tick as close to the dog's skin as you can. Be careful not to pinch the skin.

3. Slowly and steadily, pull the tick straight out. Make sure not to twist or jerk. If the tick's mouthparts remain in the skin, try to remove them with tweezers. If you have the tick remover card included in the PetVet Medic First Aid Kit, you can slide the notched edge under the tick, then gently push the card forward and upward with steady pressure to detach the tick.

4. Once the tick is removed, disinfect the bite site with rubbing alcohol or another disinfectant.

5. Place the tick in a container with rubbing alcohol. You can also flush it down the toilet.

6. Monitor the dog for any signs of infection or illness, such as a fever or lethargy. If the tick is engorged already (see photo), and you are in an area with high incidence of Lyme disease, consult with your veterinarian to determine if they would recommend testing for Lyme disease or starting a course of treatment as a preventive.

Tick-Borne Diseases

Lyme Disease

Lyme disease is a bacterial infection transmitted through the bite of a tick infected with the bacterium *Borrelia burgdorferi*.

- Dogs and humans are commonly affected by Lyme disease, especially those living in areas with high tick populations or spending a lot of time outdoors.

- It's transmitted by the **deer tick** and **Western black-legged tick**.

- Ticks that transmit Lyme disease can be found throughout the United States and Canada.

- Some dogs may not show any symptoms, while others may develop serious complications, such as kidney disease, heart disease, or nervous system problems, if left untreated.

Symptoms

Symptoms can vary but may include:

Loss of appetite	Weakness	Lethargy
Fever	Joint pain	Stiffness
Difficulty breathing	Swollen lymph nodes	

Ehrlichiosis

Ehrlichiosis is caused by *Ehrlichia* bacteria transmitted by a tick bite.

- It's more common in the Southwest and Gulf Coast areas of the United States.

- It's transmitted by the **lone star tick** and **brown dog tick** and can affect both people and pets.

Symptoms

Ehrlichia species invade white blood cells and platelets, leading to symptoms related to inflammation and blood clotting disorders.

Depression	Lethargy	Loss of appetite	Nasal discharge
Eye discharge	Nosebleeds	Reluctance to move	Lameness (not always same leg)

Rocky Mountain Spotted Fever (RMSF)

Rickettsia rickettsii bacteria transmitted through tick bites are the main cause of Rocky Mountain spotted fever. It can infect dogs and people.

- The **Rocky Mountain wood tick**, **brown dog tick**, and **American dog tick** can transmit RMSF.

- While RMSF is more prevalent in the Rocky Mountain states, it can also be found throughout the United States and Canada, particularly in the Southeast.

Symptoms

Symptoms are usually severe and last a few weeks. It can be fatal.

Fever	Stiffness when walking
Depression/Lethargy	Neurological changes

Anaplasmosis

Anaplasmosis is caused by species of *Anaplasma,* most commonly *Anaplasma phagocytophilum.* These bacteria can affect dogs and people.

Hepatozoonosis

Hepatozoonosis is caused by an infection from the parasite *Hepatozoon americanum*. It's transmitted by the **Gulf Coast tick** and **brown dog tick**.

- The parasite is transmitted when a dog ingests an infected tick. This is different from other tick-borne diseases, which require a bite from a tick to be infected.

- Cases have been reported in the mid-Southern and Eastern regions of the United States.

- It rarely affects people.

Symptoms

Hepatozoon can infect the white blood cells or muscles, depending on the species. It can cause vague, mild symptoms, or it can be potentially fatal.

Loss of appetite	Lethargy	Fever
Depression	Eye discharge	Weight loss

Prevention

Prevention is key to avoiding tick-borne disease in dogs. This can be achieved by using tick-preventive medications such as Bravecto, Seresto collars, Simparica Trio, and Revolution. You can also check your dog for ticks regularly and avoid areas with high tick populations. Since tick-borne diseases can also affect humans, it's important to protect yourself too.

Scorpions

While scorpion stings can be painful to pets and people, they're typically not dangerous. One species, however, can cause serious issues.

Arizona bark scorpion
(*Centruroides sculpturatus*)

Photo courtesy Wikipedia

- These are found in Arizona, southern Utah, western New Mexico, Nevada, and around the Colorado River in California.

- It's the only species capable of producing notable systemic effects.

- All scorpion venom is made of neurotoxins and proteins, and the Arizona bark scorpion's venom can affect the nervous system and heart.

Symptoms

Swelling	Itchiness	Pain
Crying	Limping	Drooling
Loss of balance	Twitching	Fever

Treatment

For mild stings, you can control pain, inflammation, and possible allergic reaction.

- Wash the area where the pet was stung.

- Apply cold compress/ice pack to area.

- If your pet is in pain and has been prescribed a non-steroidal anti-inflammatory (NSAID) like Rimadyl, Metacam, or Deramaxx, you can give that. Or give one dose of aspirin based on your dog's weight (see p. 144).

- To help prevent an allergic reaction, give diphenhydramine (Benadryl): 1 mg/pound (see p. 137).

- You may need to repeat the dose. You can give Benadryl every 12 hours for 2-3 days.

- If symptoms worsen, transport to the closest emergency room.

Prevention

- Keep your dog on a leash when outside.

- Keep your pet inside at night.

- Seal doors to prevent scorpions from getting inside.

Snake Bite

If your pet has been bitten by a snake, do not attempt to kill the snake or get near it. If you are not sure what type of snake it is, take a photo for the doctor. Seek immediate care with a veterinarian. If it is a rattlesnake bite, your pet may need antivenin.

Here are common venomous snakes to watch out for:

Viper (*Viperidae* family)

Viper venom contains a toxin that can destroy tissue/muscle and stop blood from clotting. Vipers in the United States include rattlesnakes, copperheads, and cottonmouths.

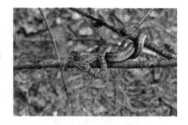

Rattlesnake (*Crotalus* spp.)

Pygmy Rattlesnake
(*Sistrurus miliarius*)

Eastern Copperhead
(*Agkistrodon contortrix*)

Cottonmouth/Water Moccasin
(*Agkistrodon piscivorus*)

Eastern Massassauga Rattlesnake
(*Sistrurus catenatus*)

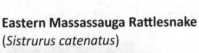

Symptoms

Swelling/edema	Limping	Pain
Vomiting	Bleeding	Bruising

Treatment

- If possible, keep your dog from moving too much; movement can cause the venom to work its way throughout the body faster.

- You can give 1 mg/pound of Benadryl (diphenhydramine), and then take your pet immediately to your vet or an ER.

Prevention

Consider getting the rattlesnake vaccination* and doing snake aversion classes if you live in an area with snakes. Also, avoid walking in areas known for rattlesnakes.

The rattlesnake vaccine doesn't eliminate the need for a veterinary visit. It means that while antivenin might still be recommended, hospitalization may not be as long.

Coral Snakes

Coral snake bites in animals are not common.

Their venom is neurotoxic with little tissue damage or pain at the bite site. Here are a few of the most common species:

Photo courtesy Wikipedia

Texas Coral Snake
(*Micrurus fulvius tenere*)

These are found in southern Arkansas, Louisiana, and eastern and west central Texas.

Eastern Coral Snake
(*Micrurus fulvius fulvius*)

These are found in eastern North Carolina, south to Central Florida, and west to Alabama, Mississippi, and eastern Louisiana to the Mississippi River.

Sonoran Coral Snake/Arizona Coral Snake
(*Micruroides euryxanthus*)

These are found in central and southeastern Arizona and in southwestern New Mexico.

South Florida Coral Snake
(*Micrurus fulvius barbouri*)

Similar to eastern coral snakes, these are found in southern Florida and the northern Florida Keys.

Symptoms

Weakness	Twitching	Respiratory failure	Paralysis

Treatment

- If possible, keep your dog from moving too much; movement can cause the venom to work its way throughout the body faster.

- Hospitalization for supportive care may be needed, along with an antivenin, if available.

- You can give 1 mg/pound of Benadryl (diphenhydramine), and then take your pet immediately to your vet or an ER.

Spiders

Most spider bites are harmless, but a few are dangerous and require immediate attention.

Brown Recluse

- It takes several days to notice symptoms of a brown recluse bite.

- The initial bite may sting, and it may blister in 2-8 hours.

- The resulting lesion may look like a target—a pale center and red outer ring.

- The bite leads to necrosis, in which the skin dies around the bite area and can be extensive.

Treatment

- No specific treatment is available.

- Apply a cool compress after bitten, and keep your pet quiet to decrease venom spread and inflammation.

- Your pet should be seen by your veterinarian if your pet is in pain or you notice darkening of the skin or a wound forming.

Black Widow

- The black widow has the most potent venom per volume.

- Symptoms from a bite occur within 8 hours.

- Death is more common in cats than dogs.

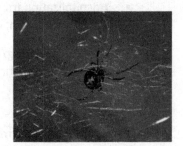

Symptoms

Moderate to severe pain	Mild redness around bite	Vomiting
Diarrhea	Muscle cramping	Agitation
Tremors	Abdominal spasms	

Treatment

- Take your pet to a veterinarian immediately.

- Antivenin is available but not commonly stocked by veterinarians.

- Your veterinarian can recommend supportive treatment for pain and side effects of toxin.

Toad Poisoning

Certain species of toads have toxins in their skin that they secrete through glands.

Cane Toad/Bufo Toad
(*Rhinella marina*)

- The cane toad can be found in Texas, Hawaii, Florida, Louisiana, and other tropical areas.

- They can grow 6-9 inches.

Colorado River/Sonoran Desert Toad
(*Incilius alvarius*)

- The Colorado River/Sonoran Desert toad can lead to severe poisonings.

- These toads can be found in California, New Mexico, Texas, and Arizona and can grow up to 7½ inches.

Toad poisonings are more common from March to September (rainy season) when breeding occurs. After rainfall, dawn, dusk, or nighttime, there's a higher chance these toads will be out.

- When a toad is licked or eaten, the toxin is absorbed through the mouth or open wounds.

- Even licking one of these toads could be life-threatening.

- Other toads in the US cause only mild signs if an animal licks them, but if they ingest the toad, it can result in drooling, vomiting, and mouth irritation.

- Toads are poisonous at all stages of life, including tadpoles and eggs.

- Drinking water from a bowl in which a toad was sitting or drinking pond water containing eggs can result in poisoning.

Symptoms

Drooling/frothing	Red gums	Pain
Pawing at mouth/vocalizing	Vomiting	Diarrhea

Progression of Symptoms

Difficulty breathing	Stumbling	Abnormal eye movements	Fluctuating heart rate
Tremors	Abnormal heart rhythm	Seizures	Death possible

Treatment

1. Rapid treatment is required. Your first priority is to immediately flush out the mouth with large amounts of running water. A hose or sink sprayer works well: point it towards the mouth opening, not towards the back of the mouth.

2. Point head downwards so water runs out and not into the mouth.

3. Rinse their mouth, face, and eyes.

4. Take your pet straight to your veterinarian for further treatment.

Chapter 15: OTC Medications and How to Administer

Over-the-counter (OTC) medications are drugs that can be purchased without a prescription and are often used to treat common ailments in pets, such as pain, allergies, and minor infections. While OTC medications can be useful in some situations, they can also be dangerous if not used properly.

Measuring & Calculating Dose

Measurement Conversions

- 1 tsp = 5 mL
- 2 tsp = 10 mL
- 1 Tbsp = 3 tsp = 15 mL
- 1 ounce = ⅛ cup
- 1 pound = 2.2 kg
- 1 g = 1,000 mg

Calculating Medication Doses

1. Weigh your dog in pounds.

2. Divide your dog's weight in pounds by 2.2 to get the kilograms (kg).

3. Multiply your dog's weight in kilograms by the recommended dose in milligrams per kilogram (mg/kg).

4. The resulting number is the recommended dosage for your pet.

For example: If your dog weighs 22 pounds, divide their weight by 2.2 to get 10 kg. If the medication has a recommended dose of 2 mg/kg, the recommended dose for your dog would be 20 mg (10 kg x 2 mg/kg).

How to Give Oral Medications

Ideally, if your pet is eating, you can put the pill in a treat-covered pocket or give with a small amount of lunch meat or peanut butter. If that is not possible, try the following:

Tablets or Capsules for Dogs and Cats

1. Use one hand with thumb on one side of the upper jaw and index finger on the other to open the mouth. Use your other hand to place the pill or tablet in the back of the throat.

2. Close their mouth, hold the head straight up, and rub the throat until they swallow.

Diagram 15.1

3. You can also blow in their face, which usually causes them to swallow.

Liquid Medications

For liquid medications, it's easier to draw it up in a syringe or turkey baster and gently insert the tip into their mouth through the side of their lip and slowly administer.

- It's found throughout the United States and Canada but is more common in the Northeast, mid-Atlantic, and north-central states as well as California.

- It's transmitted by the **deer tick** and **western black-legged tick**, the same ticks that transmit Lyme disease.

Symptoms

Depending on the species, it can infect white blood cells or platelets and cause failure of blood to clot or inflammation.

Symptoms can be vague and non-specific but may include:

Loss of appetite	Lethargy	Lameness
Reluctance to move	Neck pain	Neurological changes

Babesiosis

A species of blood-borne parasite causes babesiosis. It's typically transmitted through the bite of the **brown dog tick**.

- Some other species of *Babesia* can also be spread through blood transfusions or dog fights.

- Babesiosis is present in both the United States and Canada. Humans can also be infected.

Symptoms

Babesiosis attacks red blood cells, leading to anemia and clotting issues.

Weakness	Lethargy	Vomiting
Loss of appetite	Red or orange urine	

Allergy Medicine

Benadryl (Diphenhydramine)

Benadryl is an antihistamine that can be used for allergies and allergic reactions like bee stings (see p. 117) and anaphylaxis (see p. 79).

- A typical tablet or capsule of Benadryl contains 25 mg. Give your pet 1 mg per pound of weight every 12 hours.

- For bee stings, use every 12 hours for 2-3 days until the swelling is completely resolved.

Dog/Cat Weight	Benadryl Tablet Dose (1 mg/lb)	Benadryl* Liquid Dose (based on 12.5 mg/mL dose)
4-10 lb	¼ tablet (6.25 mg)	0.5 mL
10-20 lb	½ tablet (12.5 mg)	1 mL
20-30 lb	1 tablet (25 mg)	2 mL
Over 20 lb	1 tablet per 25 lb of body weight	2 mL per 25 lb of body weight

Make sure xylitol is not an ingredient in liquid Benadryl.

Antacid for Digestion Issues

Pepcid (Famotidine)

Antacids like Pepcid can help lower stomach acid and ease nausea. A typical tablet is 10-20 mg. The 10 mg tablets are easier to divide for smaller pets.

Dog/Cat Weight	Pepcid Dosage (0.5-1 mg/kg once or twice a day)
Up to 10 lb	0.5-2.25 mg
11-20 lb	1.1-4.5 mg
21-30 lb	2.3-6.8 mg
31-40 lb	3.4-9 mg
41-50 lb	4.5-11.4 mg
51-60 lb	5.7-13.6 mg
61-70 lb	6.8-15.9 mg
71-80 lb	8-18.2 mg
81-90 lb	9-20.5 mg
91-100 lb	10-22.7 mg

Antidiarrheal/Upset Stomach Medicine

Pepto-Bismol

Bismuth subsalicylate (17.5 mg/ml) is known by these brand names: Pepto-Bismol, Kaopectate, Diotame, Bismu-Kote, BismuPaste D, and Bismusal.

Dogs

Give dose every 6 hours up to 3 days. Stop if you notice improvement.

Dog Weight	Pepto-Bismol Dose*
10-20 lb	1-2 mL
21-40 lb	2-4.5 mL
41-60 lb	4.5-7 mL
61-80 lb	7-9 mL
81 lbs-100 lb	9-11 mL
Over 100 lb	Each additional 20 lb: add 2 mL

Bismuth can cause stool to temporarily turn black, which is normal.

Cats

Give dose every 12 hours. It is not recommended to give more than 2-3 doses total for cats.

Cat Weight	Pepto-Bismol Dose (4.4 mg/kg every 12 hours)
Up to 5 lb	0.5 mL
5-10 lb	1.1 mL
10-15 lb	1.7mL
15-20 lb	2.2 mL

Bismuth can cause stool to temporarily turn black, which is normal.

Tums

Calcium carbonate medicines, such as Tums, can add calcium for nursing pets and can be used for digestive upset. The most common size is the 500 mg tablet.

Dog/Cat Weight	Tums Dose (25-50 mg/kg each day)
10-20 lb	¼-½ tablet
20-40 lb	½-1 tablet
40-60 lb	1-1.5 tablets
60-80 lb	1.5-2 tablets
80-100 lb	2-3 tablets
Over 100 lb	Each additional 20 lb: add ½ tablet

Imodium (Loperamide)

Imodium typically comes in 2 mg tablets. Note that Imodium is not recommended in collie, Australian shepherd, Old English sheepdog, and Shetland sheepdog breeds.

Dogs

The dose is 0.1-0.2 mg/kg every 12-24 hours for up to 3 days.

Dog Weight	Imodium Dose
5-20 lb	0.25-1 mg
21-60 lb	1-2 mg
60+ lb	2-4 mg

Cats

The dose is 0.1-0.2 mg/kg every 8-12 hours for 3 days maximum.

Cat Weight	Imodium Dose
Up to 5 lb	0.25 mg
5-10 lb	0.5 mg
10-15 lb	1 mg
15-20 lb	1.25 mg

Probiotics

If you're using the probiotic Culturelle,* here is the recommended dose per day for cats and dogs:

Pet Weight	Culturelle Dose (per day)
Under 10 lb	½ capsule
10-60 lb	1 capsule
60+ lb	2 capsules

*For pet-specific probiotics, visit www.petvetproduct.com.

Constipation Relief

Metamucil

You can give 2 teaspoons of Metamucil powder with each meal, or you can give 2-3 tablespoons of bran breakfast cereal (Fiber One or All-Bran) with each meal.

Cough Suppressant

Robitussin DM

Robitussin DM contains dextromethorphan (20 mg/10 mL) to treat a cough, and guaifenesin (200 mg/10 mL) to thin mucus. Be sure that the cough medicine does not contain xylitol, which is dangerous to pets.

The doses given in the chart are for dogs only. Use every 8-12 hours as needed for cough.

Dog Weight	Robitussin DM Dose
10 lb	1-2 mL
20 lb	2-4 mL
30 lb	3-6 mL
40 lb	4-8 mL
50 lb	5-10 mL
60 lb	6-12 mL
70 lb	7-14 mL
80 lb	8-16 mL
90 lb	9-18 mL
100 lb	10-20 mL

Ear Medicine

1. While someone restrains your pet, hold up the ear flap and drop the medicine straight into the ear (don't insert too deeply or at an angle; it should be straight down).

2. Remove the tube, and while holding up the ear, massage the bottom of the ear to distribute the medicine.

Eye Medicine

1. While someone restrains your pet, hold your index finger above the eye and, using your thumb, gently roll the lower eyelid down.

2. Drop ¼ inch strip of eye lubricant (or medicine) inside the lower eyelid. Then release the eyelid and close the eye.

3. If there is no one to help restrain, it's easiest to have your pet sit down while you come from behind them. Use your thumb to position above the eye and your index finger to gently roll the lower eyelid down.

Motion Sickness/Vomiting Medicine

Meclizine

Meclizine has several brand names: Antivert®, Dramamine® Less Drowsy Formula, Bonine®, Bonamine®, Postafen®, and Univert®. It typically comes in 25 mg tablets.

Weight	Meclizine Dosage (0.5 mg/kg once a day)
Dogs <25 lb	¼ of tablet (6.25 mg)
Dogs 25-50 lb	½ of tablet (12.5 mg)
Dogs >50 lb	1 tablet (25 mg)
Cats	½ of tablet (12.5 mg)

Pain Medicine

Aspirin

Aspirin is a nonsteroidal anti-inflammatory drug (NSAID) that is sometimes used to treat pain and inflammation.

- A regular aspirin tablet is 325 mg.

- A baby aspirin has 81 mg.

- For both dogs and cats, do not give more than 2 doses without consulting your veterinarian.

Dog Weight	Aspirin Dosage*(10 mg/kg every 12 hours)
Up to 10 lb (4.5 kg)	45 mg
11-20 lb (5-9.1 kg)	90 mg
21-30 lb (9.5-13.6 kg)	136 mg
31-40 lb (14-18.2 kg)	181 mg
41-50 lb (18.6-22.7 kg)	227 mg
51-60 lb (23.1-27.3 kg)	272 mg
61-70 lb (27.7-31.8 kg)	318 mg
71-80 lb (32.2-36.4 kg)	363 mg
81-90 lb (36.7-40.9 kg)	409 mg
91-100 lb (41.3-45.5 kg)	454 mg

*Do not give aspirin if the animal is severely dehydrated, has kidney disease, or is on prednisone or any nonsteroidal anti-inflammatories, such as Metacam, Rimadyl, and Deramaxx.

Cat Weight	Aspirin Dose* (10 mg/kg every 48 hours)
Up to 5 lb (2.3 kg)	23 mg
5-10 lb (2.3-4.5 kg)	45 mg
10-15 lb (4.5-6.8 kg)	68 mg
15-20 lb (6.8-9.1 kg)	91 mg

Do not give it if the animal is severely dehydrated, has kidney disease, or is on prednisone or any nonsteroidal anti-inflammatories like Metacam. Do not give more frequently than every 48 hours, and do not give more than 2 doses without consulting a veterinarian.

Toxin-Binding Agents

If your pet consumes something poisonous, like insecticide, use a toxin-binding agent as an emergency treatment until you can get to your veterinarian.

Activated Charcoal

For both dogs and cats, activated charcoal can absorb toxins they've ingested. It will turn stools black, which is normal. Give 1-3 g/kg by mouth once, then give half the initial dose every 4-8 hours for up to 2 days. Consult your veterinarian on how many doses they need because it depends on which toxin your pet ingested.

- If you're using powdered charcoal, mix the total dose with 50-200 mL of warm tap water, and give it carefully by mouth in small doses.

- You can also mix with a canned dog or cat food.

Dog/Cat Weight	Charcoal Dose (1-3 g/kg)
10 lb (4.5 kg)	4.5-13.6 grams
20 lb (9.1 kg)	9.1-27.3 grams
30 lb (13.6 kg)	13.6-40.9 grams
40 lb (18.2 kg)	18.2-54.5 grams
50 lb (22.7 kg)	22.7-68.2 grams
60 lb (27.3 kg)	27.3-81.8 grams
70 lb (31.8 kg)	31.8-95.5 grams
80 lb (36.4 kg)	36.4-109.1 grams
90 lb (40.9 kg)	40.9-122.7 grams
100 lb (45.5 kg)	45.5-136.4 grams

ToxiBan® Charcoal-Kaolin Suspension

ToxiBan can bind most toxins. It will cause stools to turn black, which is normal. Give by mouth 5-10 mL per pound of weight.

Disinfectants to Clean Wounds

Povidone-Iodine Disinfecting Solution

- Betadine is a common brand for this disinfectant.

- It can stain your hands and clothing.

Chlorhexidine Solutions

- Hibiclens is a common brand for this disinfectant.

- These often come in spray bottles for ease of use.

Hydrogen Peroxide

It is not recommended to use hydrogen peroxide on wounds because it can delay healing and damage the tissue.

Soap and Water

This is a good way to clean out wounds, especially dirty ones.

Topical Gels & Creams

Neosporin (Triple Antibiotic Ointment)

- This is a topical antibiotic used for skin infections.

- Apply a thin layer onto the affected area every 12 hours.

- Use with caution in cats, because some cats can have a rare reaction.

Silver Sulfadiazine Cream and Silver Wound Gel

- Both of these can be used on skin burns.

- Apply a thin layer onto the affected area every 12 hours.

Cortisone Cream (Hydrocortisone)

- Topical cortisone can be used for skin irritation and allergies.

- Apply a thin layer onto the affected area every 12 hours.

How to Induce Vomiting in an Emergency Situation

- Seek veterinary care when your pet has ingested something toxic. If you are unable to seek veterinary emergency care, then inducing vomiting at home can be lifesaving.

- DO NOT INDUCE VOMITING IN CATS.

- Note that inducing vomiting is not recommended in cases involving ingesting alkalis, acids, corrosive agents, hydrocarbons, or sharp objects such as bones.

- Inducing vomiting can cause gastritis/stomach irritation, and there is a risk of your pet inhaling the irritant into their lungs.

Hydrogen Peroxide (3% only)

Make sure the peroxide isn't expired and still fizzes to be effective. Feeding a small meal, such as bread or kibble, before giving the peroxide may help its effectiveness.

1. Give your dog 1 mL/pound by mouth (do not exceed 45 mL total). Use a syringe or turkey baster if possible.

2. Walk them around after giving the peroxide.

3. You can repeat one time after 15 minutes if not successful, but **do not give your dog more than 45 mL total**.

Inducing vomiting is not recommended in certain brachycephalic breeds like bulldogs and pugs because there is a risk of aspiration pneumonia.

Do not give peroxide to cats.

Dog Weight	3% Hydrogen Peroxide Dosage (1 mL/pound)
5 lb	5 mL
10 lb	10 mL
15 lb	15 mL
20 lb	20 mL
25 lb	25 mL
30 lb	30 mL
35 lb	35 mL
40 lb	40 mL
45 lb	45 mL
50+ lb	45 mL (max dose)

Conclusion & References

This guide is intended to provide pet owners with the basic knowledge and skills to give first aid to their pets in an emergency.

However, remember that first aid is not a substitute for veterinary care, and you should always seek professional help as soon as possible.

Additionally, it is recommended that you take a pet first aid course to gain more in-depth knowledge and skills.

Remember, being prepared and knowing what to do in an emergency can save your pet's life. To purchase the premade PetVet Medic First Aid Kit, which has all the essential items you may need in an emergency, visit us at www.petvetproduct.com.

Pet Poison Helpline: (855) 764-7661

Call the Pet Poison Helpline for recommendations if your pet was exposed to anything potentially toxic.

References

Rebecca J. Eisen, and Lars Eisen. "The Blacklegged Tick, *Ixodes scapularis*: An Increasing Public Health Concern." *Trends in Parasitology*, 34(4), April 2018: 295–309. https://doi.org/10.1016/j.pt.2017.12.006.

Allen M. Schoen, *Veterinary Acupuncture: Ancient Art to Modern Medicine*, 130. St. Louis, London: Mosby, 1994.

AKC Canine Health Foundation (www.akcchf.org).

ASPCA Animal Poison Control (www.aspca.org/pet-care/animal-poison-control).

Robin Van Metre, VMD; Dennis T. (Tim) Crowe, Jr., DVM, Diplomate ACVS Emeritus, Charter Diplomate ACVECC, FCCM; KaLee Pasek, DVM; Jo-Anne Brenner, EMT-Tactical, NREMT-I, K9 MEDIC® Executive Director and Founder.

Illustrations done by Ankita M.

Index

From toxins 38-41, 43-44,
46, 48, 51-54, 58, 99, 101,
103-9, 134
From trauma 63, 70
Inducing 148
Treatment 84, 97, 143

W

Walking difficulty 34, 39, 54,
62, 68, 123

Warfarin 106

Wasp stings 117

Water

For cleaning wounds 22,
23, 26, 77, 147
For cooling 33, 57, 84
For hydration 95, 97, 105
For rinsing eye 80
For rinsing mouth 40, 100,
101, 134
For rinsing skin 88
Ocean 104
Pond 39, 134

Water moccasin 128

Weakness

From infection 122, 124
From overdose 106, 110,
112, 115, 116
From spinal injury 69
From toxins 39, 43, 51, 52,
54, 99, 131

From respiratory distress
65, 67

Weight loss 59, 63, 125

Western black-legged tick
120, 122, 124

Wheezing 65, 67, 101

Wounds

Bite 77, 78, 132
Bleeding 30
Burns 57
Cleaning 146-47
Footpad 25-26
Gunshot 61
Treatment 22-23

X

XXT (External Extraction
Technique) 9-10

Xylitol 7, 35, 54, 114, 137,
142

Y

Z

Zinc phosphide 109

Made in United States
North Haven, CT
10 December 2024

62141526R00098